# Reading CAE

## Eight more practice tests for the Cambridge C1 Advanced

**CAE**
—
**C1**

# PROSPERITY EDUCATION
www.prosperityeducation.net

Registered offices: Sherlock Close, Cambridge
CB3 0HP, United Kingdom

© Prosperity Education Ltd. 2023

First published 2023

ISBN: 978-1-915654-09-0

Cover design and typesetting by ORP Cambridge

For further information and resources, visit:
www.prosperityeducation.net

To infinity and beyond.

# Contents

# Introduction

Welcome to this second edition of sample tests for the Cambridge C1 Advanced (CAE) Reading examination (Parts 5–8).

Parts 5–8 of the Reading and Use of English section test candidates' ability in reading different types of text for detail, purpose, opinion, tone and attitude, and repeated practice of the assessment format is key to achieving a passing grade.

This resource comprises eight whole Reading tests, answer keys, write-in answer sheets and a marking scheme allowing you to score each test out of 26 marks.

The content has been written to closely replicate the Cambridge exam experience, and has undergone comprehensive expert and peer review. You or your students, if you are a teacher, will hopefully enjoy the wide range of essay topics and benefit from the repetitive practice, something that is key to preparing for this section of the C1 Advanced (CAE) examination.

We hope that you will find this resource a useful study aid, and we wish you all the best in preparing for the exam.

**Prosperity Education**
Cambridge, 2023

For more Cambridge exam-preparation materials, including free sample tests and online resources, visit www.prosperityeducation.net

# Cambridge
# C1 Advanced
# Reading

# Test 1

## Part 5

**You are going to read from an interview in which a woman named Karen Martin talks about how to become a garden designer. For questions 31–36, mark the appropriate answer (A, B, C or D) that you think fits best according to the text.**

## Becoming a garden designer

It's a fresh, crisp morning and Karen Martin is sitting in her garden. "As someone who has always had a deep appreciation for nature and its beauty," she says, "becoming a professional garden designer was a dream come true for me. I had always enjoyed spending time outdoors, working in my own garden and learning about different plant species, but it wasn't until later in life that I realised I could do it for a living." Becoming a professional garden designer can be a rewarding and fulfilling career path for those with a passion for the art of cultivating gardens. Garden designers create outdoor spaces that are both functional and beautiful, often incorporating a wide range of plants and other elements to create a unique and enjoyable environment.

"I've always enjoyed gardening, but I've always been aware from the get-go that there had to be more to it than that," says Karen, who worked in Real Estate before changing careers. "I committed to gaining a deeper understanding of the principles of design. To do that I enrolled in a difficult training program that covered everything from the basics of landscape design to more advanced topics."

Karen admits: "The program was challenging, but incredibly rewarding as I gained a new perspective of the natural world around me."

In addition to formal education, gaining practical experience is essential for developing the skills needed to be a successful garden designer. "I also spent countless hours volunteering at botanical gardens and nurseries to gain hands-on experience in the field." Karen recalls. "It was during these experiences that I learned about plant care and design, and how they interact to create beautiful outdoor spaces."

"You may consider internships or apprenticeships with established designers or landscapers in your area to gain hands-on experience with plant care and other elements of garden design. You may also want to start your own garden or volunteer with a community garden to gain experience of planting, maintenance and design," says Karen.

Those interested in becoming a landscape gardener may try building a collection of photographs, sketches or computer drawings of garden plans, and any other relevant work samples that demonstrate skills and creativity. "As I gained experience and developed my skills, I started building a catalogue of my work to show my abilities to potential clients or employers," says Karen.

One of the most rewarding aspects of becoming a professional garden designer for Karen has been the opportunity to work with clients to turn their outdoor spaces into something truly unique and beautiful.

"I love listening to my clients' visions and bringing them to life through thoughtful design and plant selection. Seeing the joy and satisfaction on their faces as they walk through their newly designed garden is an experience that never gets old." She continues: "Of course, like any profession, there are challenges that come with being a garden designer. The long hours are tiring, and the weather and soil conditions can all present obstacles to creating the perfect outdoor space. But it's these challenges that make the job all the more rewarding when you're able to overcome them and create something truly special."

"All in all, becoming a professional garden designer has been a journey of hard work, dedication and passion. It's a career that allows me to combine my love for nature with my desire to create beauty and bring joy to others. Plus, I always end up having a good night's rest due to the physical parts of the job. I wouldn't have it any other way."

**31** What does Karen say about her background in paragraph 1?

    **A** Gardening wasn't always very rewarding for her.

    **B** Designing gardens as a future career was something she didn't want to do.

    **C** Being a professional gardener was something she didn't think was possible.

    **D** Working on her own garden wasn't fulfilling enough.

**32** What did Karen learn from the training program?

    **A** A new understanding of the world.

    **B** How to conduct simple landscape design

    **C** Advanced subjects in gardening.

    **D** How to solve the many difficulties of landscape gardening.

**33** What two things are necessary to succeed in the gardening business?

    **A** Working and developing skills with other successful gardeners.

    **B** Learning how to take care of plants by starting your own garden.

    **C** Developing life skills at university and practical experience.

    **D** Obtaining a recognised education and hands-on experience.

**34** What does Karen suggest a person do to show off their work?

    **A** Focus on networking with clients or employers.

    **B** Provide appropriate work samples to potential employers.

    **C** Take photographs of gardens for inspiration.

    **D** Put together a collection of suitable examples of work.

**35** According to Karen, she's never tired of

    **A** being a professional gardener.

    **B** the climate and soil conditions.

    **C** watching a person's reaction when they see their new garden.

    **D** working outside.

**36** In the final paragraph, Karen talks about the physical aspects to her job in relation to

    **A** dedication.

    **B** sleep.

    **C** passion.

    **D** nature.

## Part 6

You are going to read four reviews of the television series 'Downton Abbey'. For questions 37–40, choose from the reviews A–D. The reviews may be selected more than once.

## Downton Abbey
## Is it really accurate?

### A

I find the TV series Downton Abbey to be an inaccurate representation of the lives of the wealthy and their servants in early 20th-century Britain. The series really romanticises the class system. Firstly, it presents an unrealistic picture of the relationship between the rich and their servants. The servants are seen as loyal and devoted, with no desire for better working conditions or higher wages. This is simply not true. Furthermore, the series completely ignores the political and social changes of the time. The early 20th century was a time of great social and political change in Britain, with the rise of the labour movement and the fight for women's rights. The series completely ignores these important historical events. Finally, I find it to be incredibly sexist. Female characters are either powerless and dependent on men, or they're horrible and mean. There are few strong female characters in the series, and those that do exist are often punished for their independence and strength.

### B

Downton Abbey is a highly enjoyable television series. It presents a fictional but historically accurate representation of people during the early 20th century. The show's attention to detail, elegant costumes and stunning settings all contribute to its realistic appeal. One of the things I appreciate most about Downton Abbey is its focus on tradition and the importance of maintaining social order. The wealthy Crawley family are shown to be responsible, and their servants are shown as loyal and dedicated to their roles. Moreover, the series explores the changing times of the early 20th century as Britain moved towards a more modern and democratic society. This is shown through the Crawley family's struggle to maintain their status and relevance in a world that is rapidly changing. The characters in the show are well-developed, with both strengths and weaknesses in evidence. The show's attention to detail is especially truthful, as well as the minor activities of daily life in a large country estate. Overall, I highly recommend Downton Abbey to anyone who appreciates quality historical dramas.

### C

If you are looking for a perfect representation of the English upper class during the early 20th century, look no further than Downton Abbey. One of the most striking aspects of the show is the vast divide between the wealthy Crawleys and their working-class staff. The show is a perfect reminder of the extreme class divide that existed during that time period. Furthermore, the show's romantic storylines are so over-the-top. The constant love triangles and forbidden passions are more of a soap opera than a period drama. It's almost as if the writers felt the need to inject as much drama as possible into the plot to keep the viewers engaged. The characters are people who we mostly love or hate, and the representation of women is a bit all over the place. We do have the hilarious Dowager Countess, who provides the humour, but many of the other women are just stereotypes. But for all its faults, there's no denying that Downton Abbey is beautifully shot. The costumes and set designs are stunning, as well as extremely realistic. It's clear that a lot of effort went into making the show as visually appealing as possible. In conclusion, Downton Abbey is a highly entertaining and well-crafted period drama that's worth watching. However, it's important to remember that it is ultimately a work of fiction.

**D**

The show connects themes of power, morality and society in a way that both engages and challenges the viewer. I found Downton Abbey to be a fascinating exploration of the human condition. At the heart of the show is the tension between the Crawley family and their servants. The relationships raise questions about the nature of power and the responsibility of those in positions of authority. The show also explores the moral obligations that come with wealth and privilege, and the consequences that can result when these obligations are ignored. Overall, Downton Abbey offers a thought-provoking exploration of power, morality and society. It challenges us to consider our own place in the world and to reflect on the moral obligations that come with privilege.

**Which person:**

| | |
|---|---|
| differs from the others regarding its focus on social and political change? | **37** |
| shares reviewer D's opinion on the show's well-written characters? | **38** |
| expresses a similar view to reviewer B regarding attention to detail? | **39** |
| shares a similar opinion to reviewer A on the representation of women? | **40** |

# Part 7

**You are going to read an extract from a newspaper article about the Rolls-Royce car company. Six paragraphs have been removed. Select from the paragraphs A–G the one that fits each gap (questions 41–46). There is one extra paragraph that you do not need to use.**

## Rolls-Royce

British company Rolls-Royce is one of the most recognisable names in the luxury automobile and engine-manufacturing industries, with a reputation for producing some of the finest and most reliable products in the world.

| 41 | |
|----|--|

Henry Royce was an engineer who had a passion for creating the perfect car, while Charles Rolls was a businessman with a keen eye for marketing. Soon after the two entrepreneurs met, they decided to create a new car company together. Their first car, the Rolls-Royce 10 HP, was produced in 1904 and was an instant success. The car was powered by a two-cylinder engine and was known for its smooth and quiet ride. Rolls-Royce quickly gained a reputation for producing cars that were among the best in the world due to their exceptional quality and craftsmanship. In 1906, Rolls-Royce introduced the Silver Ghost, a car that would become one of the most famous models in automotive history.

| 42 | |
|----|--|

During World War I, Rolls-Royce shifted its focus to producing aircraft engines for the British military. In the 1930s, the company introduced a new line of luxury cars, including the Phantom II, which was known for its modern design and powerful engine. During this time, Rolls-Royce also began to cater to the individual tastes and preferences of its wealthy customers.

| 43 | |
|----|--|

During that time, it also developed a new jet engine, the Nene, which was used in the world's first jet-powered aeroplane, the Gloster Meteor.

Rolls-Royce's success in the aerospace industry continued in the post-war period, with the company producing engines for commercial aircraft. In 1952, Rolls-Royce produced the first turbojet engine, which revolutionised the aviation industry.

The company's subsequent engines were used in a wide range of planes. In the 1960s, Rolls-Royce developed a new engine, the RB211, which was used in the Boeing 747, one of the most successful commercial aeroplanes of all time. The company was then reorganised and split into two parts: Rolls-Royce Motor Cars, which continued to produce luxury automobiles, and Rolls-Royce Limited, which focused on aircraft engines and other industrial products. The company's sales subsequently declined, and it struggled to survive. In 1971, the company was bought by the British government after it ran into financial difficulties.

| 44 | |
|----|--|

In the 1980s, Rolls-Royce faced a major challenge when it was forced to take back a large number of cars due to a mechanical problem. This was costly and damaged the company's reputation.

| 45 | |
|----|--|

One of the company's most significant successes in recent years has been the introduction of the Phantom model in 2003. This ultra-luxury sedan was designed to compete with other high-end models from companies like Bentley and Maybach, and it quickly became one of the most sought-after automobiles in the world. In the 21$^{st}$ century, Rolls-Royce has continued to innovate and expand its business interests. The company has invested heavily in new technologies, and it has explored new business models, such as car-sharing and subscription services.

| 46 | |
|----|--|

For example, the company has been involved in the production of power systems, including gas turbines and nuclear reactors.

With a commitment to quality, innovation, and customer satisfaction, Rolls Royce is well-positioned to continue its success well into the future.

**A** While Rolls-Royce cars and Rolls-Royce aeroplanes have separate owners, they still share the same name. The cars might be the most famous, but Rolls-Royce aeroplanes recently revealed a battery-powered aircraft that can reach a top speed of 387 mph.

**B** Back then, it was renowned for its superior handling, smooth ride and outstanding performance, and it quickly became a favourite among the wealthy and influential.

**C** In addition to its work in the automotive and aerospace industries, Rolls-Royce has invested in other business opportunities.

**D** However, Rolls-Royce shifted its focus once again to the aerospace industry, producing engines for military planes. This move proved to be a wise decision, as it allowed the company to diversify its business interests and establish itself as a leader in the aerospace industry.

**E** Founded in 1904 by Charles Rolls and Henry Royce, the company began producing cars that were known for their exceptional quality and engineering.

**F** Luckily, Rolls-Royce was fine by the following decade following the introduction of a number of successful models such as the Silver Seraph and the Corniche.

**G** Rolls-Royce faced a number of challenges as the automotive industry underwent significant changes. For instance, many consumers began to prefer more practical and affordable cars, and Rolls-Royce was slow to adapt to these changing trends.

# Part 8

**You are going to read a newspaper article in which five artists are discussed in reference to the history of graffiti. For questions 47–56, select the correct paragraph (A–E). Each paragraph may be selected more than once.**

**Which artist makes the following statements?**

| | |
|---|---|
| Their work was not designed to be a kind of statement. | **47** |
| They combine performance and art in their work. | **48** |
| Their art has a depressing sense of humour. | **49** |
| They are famed for their use of text and script. | **50** |
| They were one of the first to express themselves using graffiti. | **51** |
| They are able to produce work on a variety of different exteriors. | **52** |
| Their work challenges traditional conceptions of gender roles and sexuality. | **53** |
| Their job required them to travel which helped them spread their art all over the city. | **54** |
| They were one of the first to be nationally recognised as a graffiti artist. | **55** |
| They have remained unknown. | **56** |

# The history of graffiti

**A**

Cornbread, who emerged in Philadelphia in the late 1960s, is widely credited with being one of the pioneers of graffiti and was one of the first to use graffiti to spread a message. His style was characterised by large, colourful letters, and the artist is also known for his ability to climb structures, such as billboards and bridges, in order to make his work stand out even more. Cornbread was one of the first graffiti artists to use the medium as a form of personal expression. Until then, graffiti was primarily used to show names or slogans, and while he also used his 'tag' to sign his work, he was best known for creating designs that expressed his thoughts and emotions. Perhaps most notably, Cornbread was one of the first graffiti artists to achieve national attention.

**B**

In the 1970s, the New York City graffiti scene exploded, and one of the most influential artists of the era was TAKI 183. His artistic style was characterised by the use of a marker pen to write his name, usually on subway trains. Real name Demetrius, TAKI 183 was a Greek immigrant who worked as a courier, transporting goods in New York City. He used his job as an opportunity to show his name all over the city, though his signature was not initially intended to be an artistic instruction. Instead, it was simply a way for him to mark his territory and let his fellow couriers know where he had been.

**C**

Keith Haring was a graffiti artist who rose to fame in the 1980s for his distinctive style that combined elements of street art and pop art. Haring's work was also heavily influenced by his interest in dance, and his figures often appeared in motion. He quickly gained a reputation for his distinctive style and playful figures. However, unlike many other graffiti artists, Haring was not interested in simply leaving his mark on the city. He wanted to use his art to make a statement. He was deeply committed to social justice and used his art to highlight a variety of causes. He was a vocal supporter of LGBTQ+ rights, and many of his works feature homoerotic imagery that challenged conventional notions of gender and sexuality.

**D**

Banksy is one of the most famous and controversial graffiti artists of the modern era. While his true identity is unknown, his art has been exhibited all over the world, making him an international superstar. His artistic style is characterised by politics to create powerful images. Banksy's work often comments on social and political issues, such as war, consumerism and police violence. His art is also known for its dark humour, which is often used to draw attention to the strange parts of modern life. Despite many attempts to unmask the artist, his identity has remained a secret. This also allows Banksy to continue to operate outside of the general art world, and to make bold statements without fear of being caught. He often incorporates elements of production art into his pieces. For example, in 2018 he created a work called 'Love is in the Bin', which consisted of a shredded version of his famous work 'Girl with Balloon'. The piece was sold at auction for over $1 million, but as soon as it was sold, the painting was automatically destroyed. Banksy is not simply a graffiti artist, but a social commentator who uses his art to make powerful statements about the world around us.

**E**

Lee Quinones is an American graffiti artist who became famous in New York City during the 1970s and 1980s. His work often uses bold, dynamic lettering and patterns, which set him apart from other graffiti artists. Additionally, his lettering style is highly distinctive, featuring a combination of bold, sharp lines and curves that create a sense of movement and energy. Another part of Quinones' style is his ability to adapt to different environments and surfaces. Whether working on the side of a building, a train or a canvas, he is able to seamlessly integrate his designs into the surrounding space, creating a sense of harmony between his art and the environment in which it is displayed.

Name _____     Date _____

## Part 5

Mark the appropriate answer (A, B, C or D).     (6 marks)

| 0 | A | B | C | D |
|---|---|---|---|---|

| 31 | A | B | C | D |   | 34 | A | B | C | D |
|----|---|---|---|---|---|----|---|---|---|---|
| 32 | A | B | C | D |   | 35 | A | B | C | D |
| 33 | A | B | C | D |   | 36 | A | B | C | D |

## Part 6

Add the appropriate answer (A–D).     (4 marks)

| 37 | 38 | 39 | 40 |
|----|----|----|----|

## Part 7

Add the appropriate answer (A–G).     (6 marks)

| 41 | 42 | 43 |
|----|----|----|
| 44 | 45 | 46 |

## Part 8

Add the appropriate answer (A–E).     (10 marks)

| 47 | 48 | 49 | 50 | 51 |
|----|----|----|----|----|
| 52 | 53 | 54 | 55 | 56 |

# Cambridge
# C1 Advanced
# Reading

# Test 2

# Part 5

**You are going to read an interview in which a woman named Morag Giuseppe gives advice about inheritance – when you receive money and objects from someone who has passed away. For questions 31–36, mark the appropriate answer (A, B, C or D) that you think fits best according to the text.**

## Family Fortunes

Inheriting property and money can be a significant life event that brings both joy and stress to the person who receives it. Morag Giuseppe gives advice for anyone who might find themself inheriting from a family member.

When it comes to inheritance, the first thing to consider is the legal implications. In most countries, there are laws that govern inheritance, and it is essential to understand this to avoid any potential legal issues. Such laws usually determine who inherits a person's assets, how the assets are distributed and any taxes that need to be paid.

If you are the receiver of a will, a legal professional can also help you to navigate any legal issues that may arise during the process.

When it comes to heirlooms – items passed down through generations that typically have significant personal value – there are often more feelings involved. Inheriting heirlooms can be a great honour, but it can sometimes be a burden. One of the most important things to consider when inheriting heirlooms is to understand the value of the items as, if they are valuable, you may need to consider insurance or secure storage to protect them.

Another thing to consider when inheriting heirlooms is to respect the wishes of the original owner. If they had specific instructions for the items, it is essential to honour those wishes. For example, if the owner wanted a particular item to go to a specific family member or to be donated to a particular organisation, you must respect this. If the original owner did not leave any instructions for the heirlooms, it is up to the person who is given the items to decide what to do with them. In some cases, the items may be sold or donated if the receiver does not want them or cannot keep them.

If you inherit a large sum of money, it can be overwhelming. Therefore, it is essential to understand the tax implications of inheriting money. A financial advisor can help you create a plan for managing the money and will make sure that you are making wise financial decisions. One important thing to consider when inheriting money is how to use it responsibly. It is difficult not to spend the money on luxury purchases or to give it away to friends and family. However, it is essential to think about the long-term implications of these decisions. In some cases, it may be a good idea to invest the money in a retirement account or to pay off debt. This can help to ensure that the money lasts and that you are financially secure in the future.

Inheriting properties is another situation for which it is essential to understand the legal and financial implications. If the property is a home, for instance, it may be necessary to put it up for sale or rent it. If the property is land, it may be a good idea to consult with a land-management expert to determine the best use for the land. You could also give it to family or friends, but again, it is essential that you consider the impact that this may have on your relationships.

Nothing can make up for the loss of a loved one and how it affects us emotionally. However, an inheritance represents the long-lasting impact of someone. Dealing with that responsibility well shows respect for those who have gone and may make a significant difference to your situation. Being well informed therefore, should the situation arise, makes good sense.

**31** At the beginning of the text, the author advises that you should

    **A** find out for yourself about the inheritance you have gained.

    **B** identify happiness in a stressful situation.

    **C** recognise and study the laws of most countries.

    **D** understand the law to avoid legal problems.

**32** What does the author say about objects passed down through the family?

    **A** They are usually worth a lot of money.

    **B** They often cause the receiver stress.

    **C** They may need to be insured or kept safe.

    **D** They can cause people to become emotional.

**33** If the original owner of an item has no special requirements, the author suggests that you

    **A** donate to a family member.

    **B** leave it to the receiver to decide.

    **C** offer the heirloom to a charitable organisation.

    **D** give the items to a particular family member.

**34** When inheriting money, the author states that it is tempting to

    **A** treat friends and buy excessive things.

    **B** be responsible and considerate.

    **C** think about the future consequences.

    **D** pay any remaining money you owe.

**35** According to the author, what is the best course of action when inheriting housing?

    **A** Think about land management.

    **B** Understand the impact on relationships

    **C** Consider selling it or renting it out.

    **D** Give it to family and friends.

**36** In the final paragraph, what does the author say about responsibility?

    **A** It can help you stay informed.

    **B** It affects us emotionally.

    **C** It helps you deal with the overall situation.

    **D** It shows thoughtfulness for the people who have passed away.

# Part 6

You are going to read four approaches to saving the planet. For questions 37–40, choose from the approaches A–D. The approaches may be selected more than once.

## The most effective way to save our planet?

*Saving the planet is a collective responsibility, and it requires effort from individuals, corporations and governments worldwide. There are many ways in which we can contribute to protecting the environment. Here we will explore four approaches to saving the planet.*

**A**

Sustainable living is an idea that focuses on reducing our carbon footprint and minimising our impact on the environment. It involves making conscious choices about the products we buy, the food we eat and the way we live our lives. One of the essential aspects of sustainable living is energy conservation. We can reduce our energy consumption by using energy-efficient appliances, turning off lights when we leave a room and using public methods of getting around or sharing a ride to work. Another important aspect is waste reduction. This can be achieved by recycling and reducing our consumption of single-use plastics. We can also reduce our food waste by planning our meals, buying only what we need and donating excess food to those in need.

**B**

Technology and innovation are essential for saving the planet. Technology can help us find more efficient ways to use resources and reduce emissions. It can also help us develop renewable energy sources, create more efficient transportation methods and find ways to reduce waste. A particular area in which this technology can make a significant impact is transportation. Electric cars, buses and trains are becoming increasingly popular, and, as battery-technology improves, they are becoming more affordable and efficient. Self-driving cars and trucks could also revolutionise the transportation industry by reducing traffic congestion and improving safety.

**C**

Environmental activism is a crucial approach to saving the planet. It involves engaging in political action, such as campaigning for environmental regulations and supporting policies that protect the environment. It also means raising awareness and educating people about the importance of taking care of the planet. One of the most effective ways to engage in this field is to join a local or national environmental organisation. Another way to make your point is to participate in protests and demonstrations.

**D**

Lifestyle changes are essential for saving the planet. Such an approach involves each individual making conscious decisions about the products they buy, the food they eat and the way they live their lives. These changes can be challenging, but they are necessary if we want to create a sustainable future for ourselves and future generations. One of the most significant lifestyle changes that we can make is to adopt a plant-based diet. The meat and dairy industries contribute significantly to greenhouse gas emissions, and so reducing our consumption of animal products can have a meaningful impact on the environment. Following a plant-based diet can also improve our health and reduce the risk of diseases. Another lifestyle change that can have a significant impact is reducing our overall consumption. For example, being less wasteful, repairing items instead of throwing them away and buying second-hand products instead of new ones. By reducing our consumption, we can reduce our carbon footprint and conserve resources.

**Which person:**

shares A's opinion on how food and food production can help save the planet?

| 37 | |
|---|---|

expresses a similar view to approach B regarding transportation and energy consumption?

| 38 | |
|---|---|

differs from the others regarding their approach to saving the planet?

| 39 | |
|---|---|

shares a similar view to approach D on the subject of waste?

| 40 | |
|---|---|

# Part 7

You are going to read an extract from a newspaper article about Maria Montessori and her approach to education. Six paragraphs have been removed. Select from the paragraphs A–G the one that fits each gap (questions 41–46). There is one extra paragraph that you do not need to use.

## Montessori

Maria Montessori was a renowned Italian physician, educator and innovator who developed the Montessori educational model. This innovative approach to education focuses on creating a child-centered environment that encourages independent learning, creativity and critical thinking.

| 41 | |
|----|----|

Maria Montessori was born in 1870 in Chiaravalle, Italy. She was an excellent student, especially in mathematics and science. She was also interested in biology, which she later studied at the University of Rome where she became the first woman in Italy to earn a medical degree.

| 42 | |
|----|----|

In 1907, she opened her first school in Rome, known as the Casa dei Bambini (Children's House). The school was a success, and the Montessori method began to gain popularity. Montessori's motivation was to create an environment that would help children develop into independent, self-motivated learners. She believed that children learn best when they are allowed to explore and discover things for themselves. Initially, her method focused on providing a prepared environment, which included materials that would help children learn through exploration and discovery. The teacher's role in this approach was to act as a guide, rather than a traditional teacher, allowing children to learn at their own pace.

Today, the Montessori educational model is based on several key characteristics.

| 43 | |
|----|----|

The materials are also designed to be self-correcting, allowing children to learn from their mistakes without the need for help from the teacher. Another characteristic of the method is the use of mixed-age groups.

| 44 | |
|----|----|

The Montessori method also emphasises the importance of practical life skills. Children are encouraged to learn skills such as pouring, tying shoelaces and buttoning. These skills ultimately help children to develop independence. The materials used in Montessori classrooms are designed to allow children to learn through touch and movement. There is also emphasis on the importance of freedom within limits. The Montessori method approach also promotes creativity and a love of learning.

| 45 | |
|----|----|

Assessment in Montessori schools is unique in that it focuses on the individual child's progress rather than comparing them to their peers. Its approach emphasises that each child has their own unique pace of development and that they should be assessed based on their own progress. Teachers observe children as they work with materials and engage in various activities. These observations are recorded and used to track each child's progress over time. The observations also provide valuable insights into a child's interests and strengths, allowing teachers to meet each child's individual needs.

Many notable individuals have attended Montessori schools, including the founders of Google, Larry Page and Sergey Brin. They have each credited the Montessori method for their success, saying that it developed their creativity and problem-solving skills.

| 46 | |
|----|----|

It was said that the Montessori method helped them to develop confidence and independence as a child. Jennifer Aniston, the famous actress, attended a Montessori school in New York City as a child. She has credited the Montessori method with helping her develop a love of learning and a curiosity about the world.

**A** Children are put together, allowing them to learn from each other rather than how old they are. This approach also helps form a sense of community and encourages children to help each other.

**B** One of these is the prepared environment, which is carefully designed to facilitate learning. The environment includes materials that are organised and accessible to the children.

**C** As a result, the method has gained popularity worldwide and is now implemented in many schools, preschools and childcare centres.

**D** Maria wrote many books during her life, mostly in Italian. However, some were in English. You can find many of the Montessori books through the Montessori-Pierson Publishing Company.

**E** In contrast, standardised education tends to prioritise teacher-led instruction, testing and a 'one-size-fits-all' approach.

**F** Another notable Montessori graduate is the Prince of Wales, who attended the Wetherby School, a Montessori school in London, England.

**G** Maria's interest in education began when she worked as a doctor in a psychiatric hospital with children with disabilities. She observed that children with disabilities could learn if given the proper environment and tools.

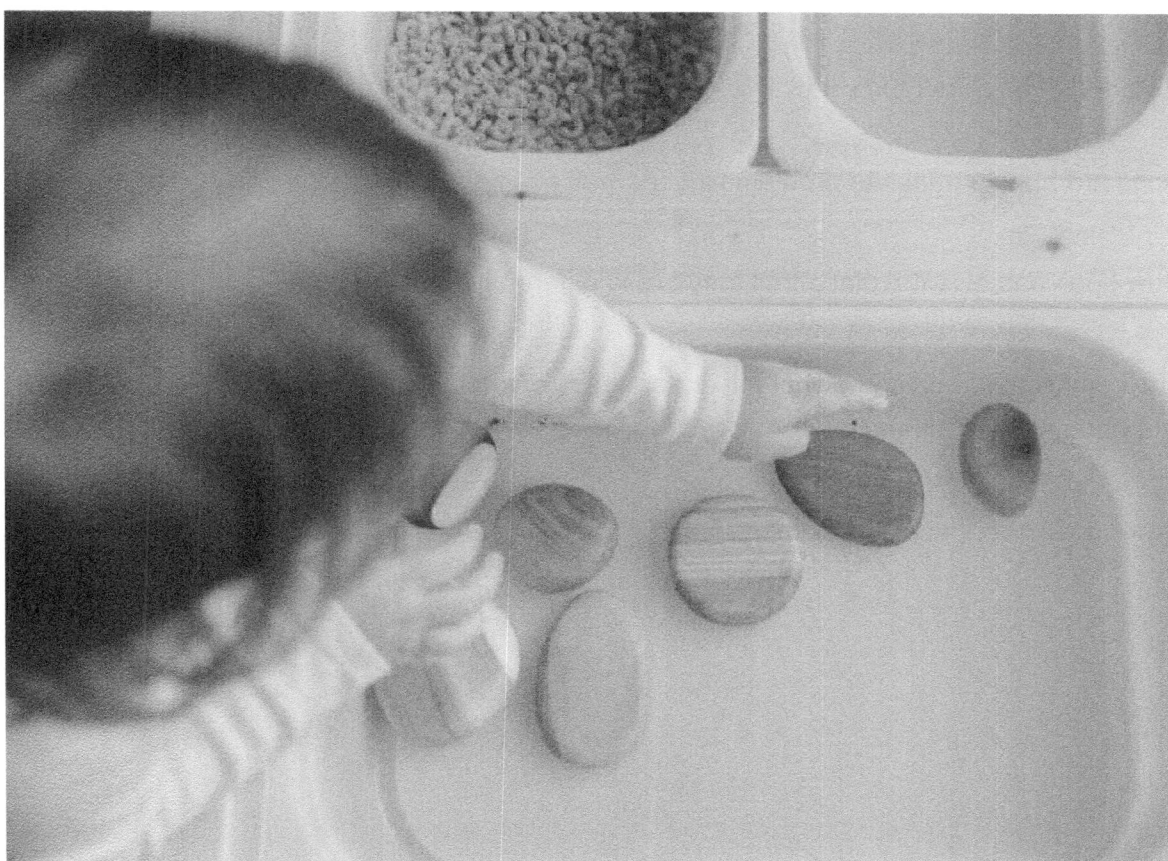

# Part 8

**You are going to read five reviews about dog books. For questions 47–56, select the correct paragraph. (A–E). Each paragraph may be selected more than once.**

**Which reviewer talks about the following things?**

| | |
|---|---|
| There are many myths about dog behaviour that will be exposed. | **47** |
| Not many animals can communicate by understanding human gestures. | **48** |
| The skills acquired when training and owning dogs. | **49** |
| Looking at a dog's ears and tail movement can help assess a dog's mood. | **50** |
| Dogs are much more than just domesticated animals, they have their own distinctive characteristics, wants and requirements. | **51** |
| How important bonding is between dogs and humans. | **52** |
| Dogs are able to translate problems just as well as infants. | **53** |
| How dogs perceive the place that they are in differently from humans. | **54** |
| The complicated and somewhat misunderstood connections that dogs and humans sometimes have. | **55** |
| How dogs experience sadness and loss. | **56** |

# Reviews of dog books

**A**

*Inside of a Dog: What Dogs See, Smell and Know* by Alexandra Horowitz is a fascinating exploration of a dog's mind. Horowitz, a scientist who specialises in dog behaviour, looks into the world of dogs, examining how they perceive the world around them and how their experiences shape their behaviour. What sets this book apart is Horowitz's engaging writing style and her use of vivid, real-life examples to illustrate her points. She draws on her own experiences as a dog owner and trainer, as well as the latest scientific research, to paint a detailed picture of what life is like from a dog's perspective. For example, Horowitz describes how her dog's behaviour changed when he was in familiar and unfamiliar surroundings, highlighting how a dog's perception of their environment is different from humans. Overall, *Inside of a Dog* is a must-read for anyone who wants to gain a deeper understanding of man's best friend.

**B**

In *The Other End of the Leash: Why We Do What We Do Around Dogs*, Patricia B. McConnell explores the complex and often misjudged relationship between humans and dogs. Through personal stories and scientific research, McConnell explains the role that body language and tone of voice play in communicating with our dog companions. She emphasises the importance of being aware of our own behaviour and the signals we are sending to our dogs, as well as understanding their natural instincts and behaviours. The book contains practical tips, such as paying attention to a dog's ear and tail position to understand their dog's mood and level of comfort.

**C**

*Bones Would Rain From the Sky: Deepening Our Relationships With Dogs* by Suzanne Clothier is a must-read for any dog lover looking to deepen their understanding of their dog companion. Suzanne Clothier's approach is based on the idea that dogs are not just pets, but individuals with their own personalities. Through personal stories, Clothier illustrates the power of connection and the joy that comes from truly understanding and respecting our dogs. In one particularly fascinating section, she explores dogs' feelings after they lose someone. Clothier shares several observations about dogs experiencing grief and mourning the loss of their loved ones, both human and canine. *Bones Would Rain From the Sky* is a deeply moving book that will inspire readers to see their dogs in a new light.

**D**

*The Genius of Dogs* by Brian Hare and Vanessa Woods is a fascinating read. The authors, both scientists, present large amounts of data that demonstrate the remarkable intelligence of our dog friends. They argue that dogs possess a unique ability to understand human communication, and that their problem-solving skills are the same as those of young children. For instance, one example of intelligence is a dog's ability to follow human pointing gestures, which is thought to be a key aspect of their ability to communicate and cooperate with humans. Few other animals are able to do this. The book covers a wide range of topics making it a comprehensive and informative read for dog lovers and scientists alike.

**E**

In *Dog Sense: How the New Science of Dog Behaviour Can Make You a Better Friend to Your Pet*, John Bradshaw presents an interesting and comprehensive exploration of the latest scientific understanding of dogs' behaviour. The book offers a fascinating look into the history of dogs and how this history has shaped their behaviour and interaction with humans. Bradshaw destroys common lies surrounding dog behaviour and offers practical advice on how to better understand and communicate with our dogs. What sets this book apart is Bradshaw's emphasis on the importance of developing a strong relationship between dogs and their owners. He argues that this is essential for the well-being of both the dog and the human.

Name _____     Date _____

## Part 5
Mark the appropriate answer (A, B, C or D).          (6 marks)

| 0 | A | B | C ▬ | D |
|---|---|---|---|---|

| 31 | A | B | C | D | | 34 | A | B | C | D |
|----|---|---|---|---|---|----|---|---|---|---|
| 32 | A | B | C | D | | 35 | A | B | C | D |
| 33 | A | B | C | D | | 36 | A | B | C | D |

## Part 6
Add the appropriate answer (A–D).          (4 marks)

| 37 | 38 | 39 | 40 |
|----|----|----|----|

## Part 7
Add the appropriate answer (A–G).          (6 marks)

| 41 | 42 | 43 |
|----|----|----|
| 44 | 45 | 46 |

## Part 8
Add the appropriate answer (A–E).          (10 marks)

| 47 | 48 | 49 | 50 | 51 |
|----|----|----|----|----|
| 52 | 53 | 54 | 55 | 56 |

© Prosperity Education Ltd. 2023 | 'Cambridge C1 Advanced' and 'CAE' are brands belonging to The Chancellor, Masters and Scholars of the University of Cambridge and are not associated with Prosperity Education or its products.

# Cambridge
# C1 Advanced
# Reading

# Test 3

# Part 5

**You are going to read an extract from an interview in which a man named Hamish MacDougal talks about national stereotyping. For questions 31–36, mark the appropriate answer (A, B, C or D) that you think fits best according to the text.**

## National stereotyping

Stereotypes are generalisations that are associated with a particular group of people or community. They are often based on limited information, although they usually have some element of truth. As a person who has lived as a foreign national in several different countries, I have met many people of different nationalities and of all shapes and sizes. So why do we stereotype, and is it fine to do so?

The study of nationalities reveals a rich source of diversity and culture, and each community has its own unique characteristics and traditions. National stereotypes can be both positive and negative in nature. Some can even prove to be offensive to the parties concerned. There is no doubt that some people find it difficult to see past stereotypes, and this definitely has an impact on society. These beliefs are often seen as harmless, humorous and even complimentary, but can still be unfair. Here are some observations of positive stereotypes:

A common stereotype is that Americans are friendly and outgoing. Americans are often seen as enthusiastic and hospitable, which is a source of pride for many Americans. This stereotype can have a positive impact on Americans, as it shows a sense of community and can lead to strong interpersonal relationships. Meanwhile, French culture is known for its grace and elegance, and this stereotype is often associated with the Parisian lifestyle. The French take pride in how they present themselves and are known for their attention to detail in all aspects of life. This stereotype can be seen as a positive aspect of French culture, as it highlights the importance of creativity.

Moving on, the Japanese are known to be hard-working and disciplined, with a strong cultural emphasis on timekeeping and dedication. This stereotype may be based on the Japanese work ethic, which values commitment. Such a stereotype can have a positive impact on the Japanese, as it provides a sense of responsibility in both personal and professional relationships. Italian culture, on the other hand, values emotion and creativity, and this stereotype is often associated with the passionate nature of Italians. This can have a positive impact on Italians, as it encourages a love for life and a sense of connection to others.

The German people are often perceived as efficient and hard-working, with a strong sense of order and organisation. This stereotype may also be based on the German work ethic, which values accuracy. This is a positive stereotype, as it shows a culture of innovation and problem-solving in which individuals work together to find solutions to complex challenges. Meanwhile, African culture is often associated with a sense of community and connection to nature. This stereotype can have a positive impact on Africans, as it creates a sense of connection to one another and to the environment. It can also lead to a culture of respect in which individuals value harmony and living with nature. Negative stereotypes, on the other hand, are beliefs or generalisations about a particular nationality that are perceived as negative or unfavourable and are often based on lies that can lead to discrimination and prejudice. For example, the notion that Germans are cold and unfriendly fails to take into account the diversity of German culture and the warmth and hospitality of many of its citizens. The stereotype of Russians often being perceived as aggressive is based on historical bias which is unfair to many Russians. Scots are often teased about being careful with money, while the English are sometimes accused of being arrogant. As this Scottish writer can confirm the modesty of my wonderful English wife, it's certainly true that many stereotypes are not accurate.

Using generalisations when identifying traits of nationalities can have a powerful impact on individuals and communities. Therefore, we must remember that each individual is unique and should be judged on their own merits. By embracing the positive aspects of these stereotypes and challenging the negative ones, we can create a more inclusive and understanding society that values diversity and celebrates the many rich cultures around the world.

**31** The writer says that while stereotypes are mostly based on false information, they usually

    **A** contain opinions that are completely true.

    **B** have some evidence related to it.

    **C** come from trusted information.

    **D** have several different dimensions.

**32** According to the second paragraph, what do people find challenging?

    **A** Going beyond the stereotype.

    **B** Understanding both positive and negative stereotypes.

    **C** Being aware of the impact that stereotypes have on society.

    **D** How they make people feel by using stereotypes.

**33** What does the writer say about time management and Japanese culture?

    **A** The Japanese are committed to keeping time.

    **B** The Japanese dedicate a lot of time to all aspects of their lives.

    **C** The Japanese value their professional lives over their personal lives.

    **D** The Japanese are known for having a strong commitment to work.

**34** According to the writer, what is mainly associated with Italian culture?

    **A** love and connection

    **B** positivity and nature

    **C** passion and innovation

    **D** encouragement and sensitivity

**35** The writer asserts that African people highly rate

    **A** strong connections with the outside world.

    **B** respect towards one another.

    **C** individual attitudes and generalisations.

    **D** innovative team-building exercises.

**36** The writer finishes by saying a sense of community can result in

    **A** controlled and unfair behaviour.

    **B** a definite influence on society.

    **C** bonds that are strong.

    **D** common generalisations.

## Part 6

**You are going to read four opinions on glamping – where people camp in luxurious accommodation compared to traditional camping. For questions 37–40, choose from the opinions A–D. The opinions may be selected more than once.**

## Glamping

**A**

I have a passion for exploring new places and experiencing different cultures. One of my favourite ways to do this is through luxury camping, also known as 'glamping'. I find that this type of travel combines the best of both worlds – the adventure of camping and the conveniences of home. Luxury camping allows me to be outside while also enjoying the finer things in life. What I love most about luxury camping is the attention to detail that goes into each experience. I enjoy waking up to the sound of birds singing and feeling the cool breeze on my face, knowing that I will spend the day exploring the great outdoors. Luxury camping also allows me to connect with nature in a comfortable way, from stargazing at night to hiking through scenic landscapes during the day.

**B**

I love to pack up my tent and hit the road, exploring new places and setting up camp in different locations. While I appreciate the comfort and luxury of glamping, my preferred way to camp is to move from place to place, rather than stay in a single location. I find that this type of camping allows me to fully experience each destination. When I go camping, I love to wake up in a new location each day, ready to explore the local area. I enjoy the challenges and the sense of adventure that come with travelling to new places. There's nothing like the unexpected events and funny little adventures that happen when you're making things up as you go along. While glamping may offer more comfort and convenience, it simply cannot compare to the sense of freedom and flexibility that comes with traditional camping.

**C**

As someone who has tried ordinary camping in the past, I can safely say that I don't like it. I find the experience to be dirty and uncomfortable. The hard work involved in camping, from moving equipment to finding a suitable spot to pitch a tent, simply isn't worth it for me. I also find the lack of comfortable items in traditional camping to be a major downside. While some may find joy in the great outdoors, I prefer to have access to basic things. But I have found a way to enjoy nature without sacrificing comfort and convenience – through glamping. I love that I can stay in one place and not have to travel around looking for 'the perfect spot'. I also love the idea of being surrounded by nature while still enjoying the comforts of home, things like a cosy bed and a private bathroom.

**D**

I find the concept of glamping to be rather horrible. To me, the point of camping is to enjoy nature by embracing the simplicity and independence of minimal comforts. Glamping, on the other hand, seems to be all about luxury and convenience. I also believe that glamping promotes a disconnection from reality. From pre-pitched tents to fancy items, glamping takes all the hard work out of camping, creating a clean and controlled version of nature. For me, the joy of camping comes from exploring the natural word, embracing the difficulties and rewards that come with it.

**Which person:**

shares D's opinion on the independence of camping?

| 37 | |

expresses a similar view to C regarding nature but also home comforts?

| 38 | |

has a different opinion than the others about moving around?

| 39 | |

shares a similar view to B on the challenges of the outside world?

| 40 | |

# Part 7

You are going to read an extract from a newspaper article about a research project on whales conducted by marine biologist Martin Brightman. Six paragraphs have been removed. Select from the paragraphs A–G the one that fits each gap (questions 41–46). There is one extra paragraph that you do not need to use.

## The Blue Whale

*Marine biologist Martin Brightman tells us about his biggest ever research project.*

During most of my career I have been fascinated by the blue whale, the largest mammal on the planet. It has been a fascinating subject for research.

For more than 30 years now I have been part of a team that explores the movements of the blue whale, including its behaviour during its lifelong journey. However, the blue whale's movement pattern is still not fully understood, so remote and extreme are the limits of its activities.

| 41 | |
|----|----|

The blue whale (*Balaenoptera musculus*) is the largest mammal on the planet and has a distinctive blue-grey skin, with lighter spots. They can grow up to 100 feet in length and weigh up to 200 tons. Despite their enormous size, these creatures feed on tiny fish.

| 42 | |
|----|----|

Blue whales are known to move between their summer feeding grounds in high latitudes and their winter breeding grounds in tropical or subtropical waters. The timing and routes of their movement vary depending on the population and the location. For example, the eastern North Pacific blue whale population, which inhabits the waters off California, Oregon and Washington, is known to travel south to breed off the coast of Mexico in the winter. The eastern North Atlantic blue whale population, which inhabits the waters off Iceland and Norway, migrates to the Azores in the winter to breed and then returns in the summer to feed.

| 43 | |
|----|----|

As a result, understanding their habits are essential to conservation efforts.

Recent technological advancements have allowed researchers to gain a better understanding of the habits of the blue whale.

| 44 | |
|----|----|

Satellite has allowed researchers to track the movements of whales across vast distances. For example, a study conducted by the Cascadia Research Collective found that the eastern North Pacific blue whales travel over 10,000 kilometres from their summer feeding grounds to their winter breeding grounds.

Other technological advancements, such as monitoring and DNA analysis, have also helped researchers to gain a better understanding of the habits of blue whales. Simply put, blue whales travel to warmer waters in the winter to breed, and then return in the summer to feed. This allows them to maximise their chances of survival. They are a protected species under international law, and thankfully its population has slowly increased since the end of commercial hunting.

| 45 | |
|----|----|

There is certainly more awareness now than when I started my career.

| 46 | |
|----|----|

Its enormous size, complex social behaviour and beautiful voice make it a truly amazing animal.

**A** The movement of blue whales is a dangerous journey with numerous hazards, as blue whales are exposed to ship strikes, fishing gear and habitat destruction.

**B** In spite of this, they are considered to be an endangered species, with only an estimated 10,000 blue whales remaining worldwide.

**C** The blue whale is the largest animal in the world. They are so big that their tongues can weigh as much as an elephant. This is probably one of my favourite facts.

**D** But through technological advancements we can understand its behaviour, including routes, timings and potential reasons for its movements.

**E** They also require a lot of food and must travel great distances to find enough food to survive. It is in these journeys that we find the best opportunity to monitor these kings of the sea.

**F** One such advancement is a technology that involves attaching a small device to the whale, which can then be tracked.

**G** Even after many years in the field, I am still thrilled to witness a blue whale come out of the ocean for some air before diving to the depths again.

# Part 8

You are going to read a magazine article in which five people talk about their experiences of working for themselves. For questions 47–56, select the correct paragraph (A–E). Each paragraph may be selected more than once.

**Which person talks about:**

| | |
|---|---|
| making contacts with people in the same trade and acquiring work from that? | **47** |
| figuring out how to manage both work and home? | **48** |
| taking on a number of roles at work? | **49** |
| spending a lot of time searching online for jobs? | **50** |
| starting with a small amount of money and a personal computer? | **51** |
| working with people from different countries? | **52** |
| hiring and keeping skilled staff members? | **53** |
| often spending the night in their place of work? | **54** |
| enjoying the relaxed atmosphere and silence? | **55** |
| their job being traditionally important? | **56** |

# Working for yourself

**A**

My journey began with a passion for fashion and a desire to create a unique brand that would stand out in a highly competitive market. I spent countless hours researching, designing and networking to turn my vision into a reality. In the beginning, it was just me, my laptop and a small budget, but with hard work and determination I was able to launch my business. One of the most significant challenges I faced as an entrepreneur was finding a balance between work and life. It's easy to get caught up in the day-to-day operations of the business and forget about other aspects of life. It is not easy. It takes hard work, and a willingness to take risks. The journey is challenging, but the reward is worth it.

**B**

I own and run a small business in the manufacturing industry in the city of Birmingham in the UK. It's not easy to run a business, employ people and be self-employed in today's economic climate, and it is even more challenging to compete with larger companies in the industry. One of the most significant difficulties I have faced is finding and holding onto skilled employees. It is crucial to have a competent workforce that can operate the machinery, produce quality goods and provide excellent customer service. However, finding workers with the right skills and experience has become increasingly difficult in recent years. Many workers in the manufacturing industry have retired or moved into different fields. I have to wear many hats and deal with numerous responsibilities. I am responsible for marketing, sales, accounting and human resources, to name just a few.

**C**

As a self-employed IT specialist living in India, I have had the opportunity to work with clients from around the world. One of the benefits of being a self-employed IT specialist is the freedom to choose my projects and work on my own terms. This has allowed me to develop my skills in areas that interest me and gain experience in diverse fields. However, it also requires discipline and self-motivation, as I am responsible for managing my workload and meeting deadlines. The flexibility of remote work has allowed me to explore opportunities beyond my local network and collaborate with clients from different parts of the world.

**D**

I'm a flamenco musician living in Spain. One of the ways that I find work is through the connections I have made within the industry. Networking and building relationships with other musicians, promoters and venue owners has been crucial in securing jobs. Being part of the flamenco community has allowed me to create a network of contacts that I can rely on for work opportunities. As a self-employed musician in Spain, I am required to register with the Spanish Social Security system. This can be a complex and time-consuming process, but it is essential to ensure that I am covered for social security benefits and can access healthcare. Despite the challenges, being a self-employed flamenco musician is a rewarding experience. Flamenco is an essential part of Spanish culture, and there is a high demand for live performances at weddings, events and festivals.

**E**

I'm a self-employed truck driver in the US. When I'm not driving, I spend a lot of time on the transportation website where I find work – jobs that suit my schedule and preferences. I carefully review the job details, such as the type of goods, distance and delivery deadline, to ensure that I can meet the client's requirements. Once I find a job that interests me, I place a bid, stating my price and availability. When I have won the bid for a job, I pick up the goods from the client's location and start my journey. I drive a lot and can spend all day driving through highways and city roads. I try to line up jobs that I can start from close to the delivery location of the previous job. It's quite common for me to sleep in the cab of my truck. It's very luxurious really, and I like the peace and quiet.

Cambridge C1 Advanced Reading | Answer sheet

Name _____     Date _____

## Part 5
Mark the appropriate answer (A, B, C or D).  (6 marks)

| 0 | A | B | C | D |
|---|---|---|---|---|

| 31 | A | B | C | D |    | 34 | A | B | C | D |
|----|---|---|---|---|    |----|---|---|---|---|
| 32 | A | B | C | D |    | 35 | A | B | C | D |
| 33 | A | B | C | D |    | 36 | A | B | C | D |

## Part 6
Add the appropriate answer (A–D).  (4 marks)

| 37 | 38 | 39 | 40 |
|----|----|----|----|

## Part 7
Add the appropriate answer (A–G).  (6 marks)

| 41 | 42 | 43 |
|----|----|----|
| 44 | 45 | 46 |

## Part 8
Add the appropriate answer (A–E).  (10 marks)

| 47 | 48 | 49 | 50 | 51 |
|----|----|----|----|----|
| 52 | 53 | 54 | 55 | 56 |

# Cambridge
# C1 Advanced
# Reading

# Test 4

# Part 5

You are going to read an extract from an interview in which a woman named Dr. Sarah Johnson talks about treating sleeping disorders. For questions 31–36, mark the appropriate answer (A, B, C or D) that you think fits best according to the text.

## Treating sleeping disorders

Insomnia – where you have difficulty sleeping – is a sleep disorders which affects millions of people worldwide. Dr. Sarah Johnson, a sleep specialist and researcher, helps us to learn more about sleep disorders and the progress being made in understanding and treating them...

I became a sleep specialist because of my own struggles with sleep. As a young adult, I had difficulty falling asleep and staying asleep, and often felt tired and annoyed during the day. I saw several doctors who provided me with medicine, but I found that it only helped temporarily and had negative side effects. Eventually, I sought out a sleep specialist. I found this area of medicine fascinating. After completing the therapy my sleep improved dramatically, and I felt like a new person. Inspired by my own experience, I decided to become a sleep specialist to help others who were struggling with sleep disorders.

Insomnia involves difficulty falling or staying asleep or waking up too early and not being able to fall back asleep, and can be caused by a variety of factors, including stress, anxiety, depression, medicine and caffeine, and environmental factors such as noise or light. It can also be a symptom of other medical conditions, such as sleep apnoea or 'restless legs syndrome'. For some of my patients, I may perform a physical exam or order tests to rule out other medical conditions that may be contributing to their lack of sleep. In other cases, a sleep study may be recommended to monitor a person's sleep patterns. I might ask them to think about the position they are in when they fall asleep and wake up,

There are several treatments available for sleep disorders, including lifestyle changes, medicine and therapy. Lifestyle changes such as establishing a regular sleep schedule, avoiding caffeine and alcohol, and creating a comfortable sleep environment can often improve sleep. Medicine such as sleeping pills may also be prescribed, but they should be used with caution and only under the guidance of a doctor. Therapy has also been shown to be an effective treatment for sleeping disorders. Such treatments, where behaviour is addressed to change the effects on a person, are preferable to drugs that only treat the symptom.

There have been several studies on the relationship between sleep disorders and other health conditions. For instance, a study published in the *Journal of Sleep Research* in 2019 found that individuals with sleep problems, particularly those who had trouble falling asleep, were at an increased risk of heart and other diseases.

One common myth is that a lack of sleep is just a normal part of ageing. While it is true that sleep patterns may change as we age, sleeping less is not a normal part of the ageing process. Another myth is that sleeping disorders can be cured with medicine. While this may help with short-term sleep problems, it is not a long-term solution and it can have negative side effects if used improperly. Therapy and lifestyle changes are often more effective in treating sleeping disorders.

If you have difficulty sleeping, I recommend talking to your doctor. From there, your doctor can work with you to develop a treatment plan that may include lifestyle changes, therapy or medicine. It is important to remember that there is no 'one-size-fits-all' solution, and it may take some time to find the treatment that works best for you. However, with the right treatment and support it is possible to improve your sleep and overall quality of life.

**31**  What does the writer say about the medicine prescribed to her?

  **A**  It taught her more about insomnia.

  **B**  It made it difficult for her to stay asleep.

  **C**  The long-term effects were not substantial.

  **D**  It made her feel sleepy and irritated.

**32**  The writer says that a lack of sleep can also be an indication of

  **A**  poor sleep positions.

  **B**  too much stress.

  **C**  unsuitable surroundings.

  **D**  further medical problems.

**33**  What advice does the writer give when talking about prescribed medicine?

  **A**  It should only be used under the supervision of a doctor.

  **B**  It can lead to more problems.

  **C**  It is better than therapy.

  **D**  It can help with overall lifestyle changes.

**34**  According to the writer, much research has been conducted on

  **A**  health conditions and their connection to sleeping disorders.

  **B**  the difficulties of falling asleep.

  **C**  diseases in relation to different types of people.

  **D**  the link between staying asleep and waking up.

**35**  What does the writer highlight as false information?

  **A**  That sleep patterns change all the time.

  **B**  Sleep disorders stem from getting older.

  **C**  Medicine can help with insomnia for an extended period of time.

  **D**  Sleep disorders can be treated with therapy and life changes.

**36**  What is meant by the phrase 'one-size-fits-all' in the final paragraph?

  **A**  There isn't an option and everyone should do the same thing.

  **B**  There isn't currently a treatment for insomnia.

  **C**  There isn't a suitable answer for everyone or for every purpose.

  **D**  There isn't a list of helpful options to help treat sleep disorders.

# Part 6

**You are going to read four tips on effective studying. For questions 37–40, choose from the tips A–D. The tips may be selected more than once.**

## Top Tips for Effective Studying

### A

Create a study schedule that works for you. This will help you to manage your time better and ensure that you cover all the necessary topics. Plan your study sessions like lessons in a school day, where you dedicate time to one topic, and change it up. It is essential to allow time for the brain to digest information before returning to it and building on the previously acquired knowledge. Taking regular rests can help you stay focused and avoid exhaustion. Try the Pomodoro technique, where you study for 25 minutes and take a five-minute rest, and then repeat. You can even try your own variations to this approach. Instead of just reading and taking notes, use active studying techniques like summarising, outlining and creating flashcards to help you remember the  information better.

### B

Note-taking strategies can help you to remember things and pass your exams. Use headings and numbering to organise your notes. This will allow you to review them easily later on and will make them easier to recall in your memory. However, be selective in your highlighting and in your notetaking. Don't try to write down everything your teacher or professor says. Focus on the main points and important details. Some people also use mnemonics, phrases formed where each letter represents something you need to remember. I tend to avoid this though, as for me they can also be confusing. Finally, I rarely take breaks. I get distracted easily so I find varying my activities better than giving myself time to do nothing.

### C

Reading effectively is crucial for understanding information, and there are some really effective reading strategies to consider. For instance, before you start reading, quickly look at the headings, subheadings and the words in bold. This will help you to get a sense of what the text is about. That being said, make sure that you then read it again properly, carefully reading any tricky points when appropriate. Summarise key points as you go. You might write a mind map or take notes to do this. For me, I found that taking breaks while revising can help me to stay focused and avoid exhaustion. I try to take a break every 45–50 minutes for 10–15 minutes.

### D

An important skill for academics and life in general is the ability to remember things easily. I would definitely recommend using mnemonic devices. These are memory aids that help you to remember information by associating it with something else. Examples include using word-building and visual imagery. Also, use repetition. Repeat the information you want to remember until it sticks. Finally, try to copy your school routine, at home. For instance, use self-testing to see your progress. This can help you to identify areas that you need to work on, and it will reinforce your memory. You can find lots of quizzes online, or you can even write your own. You'd be surprised by how much you forget from one day to the next, so write your own quiz as a review of what you have learned and test yourself the next day.

**Which person:**

expresses a similar view to C on the importance of taking breaks?   | **37** |

has a different opinion from D regarding the use of memory techniques?   | **38** |

has a similar view to B on going over work at the end of the day?   | **39** |

shares A's opinion on imitating school schedules?   | **40** |

# Part 7

You are going to read an extract from a newspaper article about the television show 'Around the World in 80 Days'. Select from the paragraphs A–G the one that fits each gap (questions 41–46). There is one extra paragraph that you do not need to use.

## Around the World in 80 Days

'Around the World in 80 Days' is a BBC TV travel series that came out in 1989.

The show followed the adventures of Michael Palin as he attempted to travel around the world in 80 days with no aeroplanes.

| 41 | |
|----|--|

The show was produced in a cultural and technological context that was very different from that of today. In the late 1980s, the world was still divided by the Cold War, and the internet was still very new. The programme was produced on film, which meant that the crew had to carry heavy cameras and equipment with them as they went.

| 42 | |
|----|--|

Palin reflected on the experience of making the show, saying: "I can honestly say that it was one of the best experiences of my life. It was tough at times, but the challenge of travelling around the world without using aeroplanes was incredibly rewarding."

One of the things that made the show so successful was Palin's enthusiasm for travel. He was always eager to try new things, new food and meet new people. Throughout the show, Palin visited a variety of different countries and experienced a wide range of different cultures and cuisine.

| 43 | |
|----|--|

It was very important to him to experience different cultures first-hand: "I think it's so important to try to understand different cultures and ways of life. It's easy to judge people from a distance, but once you actually spend time with them and see things from their perspective, you realise that we're all just human beings trying to get by in the world."

Despite the fact that the show was made over 30 years ago, it still connects with audiences today. The show is a reminder that there is so much to see and learn in the world, and that travel can be a wonderful experience.

| 44 | |
|----|--|

Another thing that made 'Around the World in 80 Days' stand out was its focus on local cuisine. Palin was always eager to try new foods and flavours, and the show featured many scenes of him sampling local items.

| 45 | |
|----|--|

Throughout the show, Palin encountered many challenges and obstacles, from tackling mountain roads in Peru to dealing with corrupt officials in China.

| 46 | |
|----|--|

The show is a reminder of the power of travel to broaden our horizons and enrich our lives, and it continues to inspire new generations to get out there and explore the world for themselves.

**A** Despite these challenges, the show was a massive success, and Michael Palin quickly became very well-known.

**E** As well as travelling, Michael Palin is famous for being part of the British comedy group Monty Python. He was also honoured by the Queen for services to travel and culture in 2019.

**B** It quickly became a cultural phenomenon and is still regarded as one of the best travel shows of all time.

**F** Reflecting on the show, Palin has said: "I think people still enjoy watching it because it's a reminder that there's a big wide world out there waiting to be explored. I hope the show inspires people to get out there and explore the world for themselves."

**C** "It is such an important part of any culture. I always make a point of trying local dishes when I travel, even if they're something I wouldn't normally eat."

**G** From the deserts of North Africa to the jungles of South America, Palin was always eager to experience the local way of life.

**D** "I think the best thing to do is to stay calm and flexible. You have to be willing to adapt to changing circumstances and be open to new experiences. Sometimes things don't go according to plan, but that's part of the adventure."

## Part 8

You are going to read a magazine article in which five people talk about working in a London museum. For questions 47–56, select the correct paragraph (A–E). Each paragraph may be selected more than once.

**Which person:**

| | |
|---|---|
| discusses one of the biggest, most thorough museums of its kind? | 47 |
| refers to a museum that is more interested in displaying creativity? | 48 |
| mentions being located in a historically converted building? | 49 |
| talks about a museum that is both educational and family-friendly? | 50 |
| mentions a museum that has a wide selection of artists of varying popularity? | 51 |
| discusses a museum that isn't as familiar as the others? | 52 |
| talks about a range of creative objects that covers thousands of years? | 53 |
| says there is a museum that tries to make science and the natural world as real as possible? | 54 |
| says that the museum's collection of bones is notable? | 55 |
| discusses a museum with historical dress and guns on display? | 56 |

# Visit a museum in London

**A**

If you're looking for a fascinating and educational experience in London, the Natural History Museum is a must-visit destination. This museum specialises in natural history and science, with a collection of over 80 million items. Among the most notable items in the collection are the skeletons, including the Diplodocus dinosaur in the main hall, as well as the blue whale and other large mammals. The museum also has an extensive collection of precious stones and interactive exhibits that bring the world of science and nature to life. The museum is open every day from 10:00 AM to 5:50 PM, and admission is free for all visitors.

**B**

If you're interested in exploring the world of art and design, The Victoria and Albert Museum is the perfect destination for you. This world-famous museum specialises in decorative arts and design, and has a collection of over 2.3 million objects all from various time periods. Among the most notable items in the collection are the Renaissance sculptures, including the sculpture of David by Michelangelo, as well as a stunning collection of fashion and textiles from around the world. With its diverse and rich collection, it provides a unique opportunity to explore the evolution of human creativity and design. The museum is open every day from 10:00 AM to 5:45 PM, with late-night openings on Fridays until 8:00 PM. Admission is free, although some special exhibitions require tickets that can be purchased online or on-site.

**C**

The Science Museum in London is a world-famous institution that celebrates the history and future of scientific innovation. With over 300,000 items in its collection, it's one of the largest and most comprehensive science museums in the world. The museum specialises in interactive exhibits that allow visitors to experience science first-hand. Notable items in the collection include the oldest surviving steam train. The museum also features interactive galleries that explore cutting-edge technologies, and there is a wide range of temporary exhibits and events to experience. It is these engaging exhibits and interactive displays that provide a unique opportunity to learn about the history and evolution of science and technology. The museum is open every day from 10:00 AM to 6:00 PM, and admission is free for all visitors.

The museum also offers a range of workshops and educational programs for children and adults, making it an ideal destination for school groups and families.

**D**

One issue that The Wallace Collection suffers from is its relatively low profile when compared to other museums in London. So, if you're looking for a hidden diamond in London's museum scene, The Wallace Collection is it. This unique museum specialises in decorative arts, with a focus on 18th-century French paintings, furniture and porcelain. Notable items in the collection include masterpieces by renowned artists such as Titian, Rembrandt and Velázquez, as well as a stunning collection of military clothing and weapons from around the world. The Wallace Collection appeals to a wide range of people, and provides a fascinating insight into the art and culture of Europe in the 18th and 19th centuries. The museum is open every day from 10:00 AM to 5:00 PM, and admission is free.

**E**

Located in the heart of London, The Tate Modern is one of the most popular contemporary art museums in the world and features a wide range of artworks from different cultures and time periods. The museum is located in a former power station on the bank of the River Thames and offers a unique and stunning architectural experience. The museum is home to many famous artists, including Pablo Picasso, Salvador Dali and Andy Warhol, as well as many lesser-known artists. The Tate Modern is open every day from 10:00 am to 6:00 pm. The museum currently has several workshops and special exhibitions available. Visitors are advised to check the museum's website before booking their tickets.

Name _____     Date _____

## Part 5
Mark the appropriate answer (A, B, C or D).                    (6 marks)

| 0 | A | B | C | D |
|---|---|---|---|---|

| 31 | A B C D | | 34 | A B C D |
|----|---------|---|----|---------|
| 32 | A B C D | | 35 | A B C D |
| 33 | A B C D | | 36 | A B C D |

## Part 6
Add the appropriate answer (A–D).                    (4 marks)

| 37 | 38 | 39 | 40 |
|----|----|----|----|

## Part 7
Add the appropriate answer (A–G).                    (6 marks)

| 41 | 42 | 43 |
|----|----|----|
| 44 | 45 | 46 |

## Part 8
Add the appropriate answer (A–E).                    (10 marks)

| 47 | 48 | 49 | 50 | 51 |
|----|----|----|----|----|
| 52 | 53 | 54 | 55 | 56 |

# Cambridge C1 Advanced Reading

# Test 5

## Part 5

**You are going to read an extract from an interview in which a man named Bill Richers talks about the music industry. For questions 31–36, mark the appropriate answer (A, B, C or D) that you think fits best according to the text.**

## Battle of the bands

As an executive with several decades of experience in the industry, I have witnessed significant changes in the music landscape over the years. When I started out in the early '80s we made great records and people purchased what they liked from the local record shop. It's true that there was a piracy issue even back then, which means people were copying music from records or the radio and reselling them. Manufacturers of music-playing devices had started producing systems that could copy records to tape and record on the radio. Even though it was technically illegal, people were able to make 'pirate recordings'. The quality of these recordings was noticeably poorer than the original, but people put up with that since they were effectively obtaining the recording for free.

Then, CDs came along and made the reality of copying files, with no noticeable change in quality, a bigger problem. With the arrival of the internet some years later, music started to be shared online on sites such as Napster. These unregulated sites presented a very real problem for performing-rights societies as well as record companies: how could they continue to control the industry? This in turn has created a problem for fresh talent in the music industry: how can bands make themselves appealing to the public, and how can they make money in the new music industry? Digital media has completely transformed the way in which music is created, distributed and consumed, and has led to new opportunities and challenges for those new bands.

In the past, the only way to achieve success was by getting signed by a major record company. However, due to the rise of digital media, bands can now upload their music to various online platforms and build support without needing a record company. One of the most important things a band can do to make it in the modern era is to be 'seen' online. For instance, social media has become a tool for musicians to connect with the people that like and follow them, and promote their music, brand and themselves. Artists can also use social media platforms like TikTok, Instagram and YouTube to create content that shows their personality and creativity, which can attract new fans and generate interest in their music. They can also show off their unique sound and style by regularly posting updates.

With the rise of the internet, bands can now distribute their music to a global audience and reach millions of potential fans. It's important for bands to make their music available on all the major platforms, like Spotify, Apple Music and Tidal, to establish a strong online presence. Yet, live performances are still a crucial part of the music industry, and they provide an opportunity for bands to directly build a connection with fans and demonstrate their talent. It also helps build a fan base and a relationship between the fans and the musicians, which can help bands make money long-term. Merchandise such as t-shirts and posters can be regularly promoted online and provide a significant source of income for bands and artists, which online services cannot provide. Merchandise can also be regularly updated to be released with new albums, tours and songs.

Finally, it's important to remember that success in the music industry takes time, and it's rare for a band to achieve overnight success. Musicians need to be patient and persistent, and they must be willing to put in the hard work and dedication required, and be prepared to take risks to stand out. They must consider the financial side of things early on and think about what they need to invest in themselves to get where they want to be. If they can surround themselves with a supportive network of people who encourage them from the start of their journey, they'll find everything else much easier to handle.

**31** According to the writer, people tolerated poor-quality recordings because

    **A**   they were against the law.

    **B**   they were great records.

    **C**   they didn't cost any money.

    **D**   they wanted to resell them.

**32** What does the writer say about the internet in relation to new musicians?

    **A**   It is difficult for them to be powerful in the industry.

    **B**   It is more difficult to make a living.

    **C**   It makes copying samples of music much easier.

    **D**   It makes the quality of sound a much bigger problem.

**33** According to the writer, if a band wants to succeed in the current market, they must

    **A**   have an online presence.

    **B**   use the internet creatively.

    **C**   have the support of a record company.

    **D**   get as many fans as possible.

**34** The writer refers to social media as

    **A**   better than having a personality.

    **B**   the only way to get signed by a record company.

    **C**   a unique opportunity.

    **D**   a device that can link musicians to their fans.

**35** What does the writer say about live performances and earnings?

    **A**   Live performances can generate a permanent income.

    **B**   Live performances help to show how talented a band can be.

    **C**   Live performances are a good opportunity to meet fans.

    **D**   Live performances help streaming services make money.

**36** In the final paragraph, the writer says that to be successful, musicians should

    **A**   invest as much money as possible at the start of their career.

    **B**   do whatever it takes to be noticed.

    **C**   have a community of encouraging artists in a similar position.

    **D**   accomplish as much as possible quickly.

# Part 6

You are going to read four reviews of the book *The Lantern Lady*. For questions 37–40, choose from the reviews A–D. The reviews may be selected more than once.

## *The Lantern Lady* by Joyce Heathburn

### A

Although I initially enjoyed the first few chapters, overall this is a tedious and uninspiring novel that fails to live up to its potential. The book tells the story of a powerful Chinese woman who is determined to maintain control over her family's business empire. Unfortunately, the promise of a gripping family story never gets anywhere. The author's attempts to create a complex character in the form of the lantern lady fall flat, as the character is just a typical Asian female stereotype. Furthermore, the book's use of Chinese cultural references feels unnatural. As a result, it reads like a dry and repetitive business manual. The plot itself is slow-moving, with little in the way of engaging storylines or character development. *The Lantern Lady* is a poorly written and disappointing novel that I would not recommend to anyone looking for an engaging read.

### B

Joyce Heathburn's *The Lantern Lady* is a sprawling family drama that explores the world of Chinese business and culture through the eyes of one family's struggles for power and control. While the book's detailed descriptions of business dealings and power struggles may be fascinating to some readers, others may find them overwhelming and difficult to follow. The main character is a powerful and interesting figure, but her personality at times feels too simple and lazy. Heathburn's writing is elegant and precise. However, the story's lack of pace and lack of action may put off those readers looking for a more exciting read.

### C

I recently read Joyce Heathburn's *The Lantern Lady*. In my view, it is a powerful novel that explores Chinese business and culture from the viewpoint of one powerful family. The main character is an interesting woman, with large amounts of intelligence and determination. The author's writing is very detailed with a deep and thorough understanding of Chinese culture, traditions and history. The book is a must-read for anyone who loves rich characters and powerful, thought-provoking narratives. However, at times the book felt overly detailed. This sometimes left me a little bored as I was more interested in the family drama rather than the minor details of every character.

### D

This amazing tale shows the finer points of Chinese business and culture. The book's detailed descriptions of business situations and power struggles are informative, but it is not something that I enjoy reading about. The lantern lady herself is a fascinating and complex figure, and is definitely more interesting than Chinese business. The book's richly detailed world-building and elegant writing style make for a memorable and engaging read. The author's deep understanding of Chinese culture and history is evident throughout the novel, and the book's vivid depictions of Chinese culture and history are nice but again a little boring. However, it does transport the reader to a world that is both exotic and familiar. *The Lantern Lady* is a well-written and informative read that will appeal to those with an interest in Chinese culture and business, but it may leave others wishing for a more emotionally engaging story.

**Which person:**

expresses a similar view to A regarding the representation of the main character?

| 37 | |

has a similar view to D on how the book is knowledgeable about Chinese culture and history?

| 38 | |

has a different opinion than the others on the book as a whole?

| 39 | |

shares A's opinion on how the book is a slow read?

| 40 | |

# Part 7

**You are going to read an extract from a newspaper article about a small island called Vanuatu. Six paragraphs have been removed. Select from the paragraphs A–G the one that fits each gap (questions 41–46). There is one extra paragraph that you do not need to use.**

## Vanuatu

Vanuatu is a small island nation located in the South Pacific Ocean, east of Australia, north of New Zealand and west of Fiji. It is an archipelago consisting of 83 islands, with a total land area of approximately 12,190 square kilometres. That makes it about 20 times smaller than the UK.

| 41 | |
|---|---|

The low-lying Pacific Island nation is a fascinating study in international conservation action. One of the most notable contributions that Vanuatu has made to conservation is its role in promoting the concept of 'cultural conservation'. This idea recognises that native cultures and their traditional knowledge are often intimately connected to the natural world, and that preserving these cultures is essential for effective conservation. Vanuatu's efforts in this area have been widely recognised, and the country has been celebrated as a model for other nations to follow.

| 42 | |
|---|---|

The country has established a number of protected areas, including the world's first shelter for sharks. These efforts have helped to protect the marine life that surrounds Vanuatu's islands, which are home to a diverse range of species including sea turtles, dugongs and various species of sharks and rays. Vanuatu has also been a supporter of stronger international action on climate change. The country is particularly vulnerable to the impacts of global warming, including rising sea levels and increasingly frequent and severe storms.

| 43 | |
|---|---|

In March 2023 a United Nations decision was adopted to make it easier to hold polluting countries legally responsible for failing to tackle the climate emergency, in a vote that has been called a historic victory for climate justice. Ishmael Kalsakau, prime minister of Vanuatu, said in a statement: "Today we have witnessed a win for climate change. Today's historic decision is the beginning of a new era in climate cooperation, one that is more fully focused on following the rule of international law, and an era that places human rights at the front of climate decision-making."

Looking back on Vanuatu's history, there have been several significant events that have impacted the country's conservation efforts. One of the most notable was the devastating Cyclone Pam, which hit Vanuatu in 2015. The cyclone caused widespread damage to the country's infrastructure, including its conservation areas and cultural sites.

| 44 | |
|---|---|

Looking forward, Vanuatu's conservation challenges are likely to only get worse in the coming years. Climate change is expected to continue to have a major impact on the country's natural and cultural assets, while unsustainable development and other human activities pose several threats. However, through partnerships with organisations such as the United Nations Development Programme, the World Bank and the Global Environment Facility, Vanuatu has been able to access additional resources and expertise to support its conservation efforts. Rather than relying solely on traditional mass-market tourism, the government has been working to develop more sustainable forms of tourism to make money.

| 45 | |
|---|---|

The success of Vanuatu's conservation efforts will depend on the continued commitment and support of its people and leaders, as well as the broader global community.

| 46 | |
|---|---|

Through its cultural conservation efforts, marine conservation initiatives on climate change, Vanuatu has demonstrated that even small island nations can have a big impact on the global conservation agenda.

**A** As the world faces increasingly urgent environmental challenges, it is essential that nations like Vanuatu continue to play a leadership role in promoting conservation and sustainable development.

**B** Despite its small size and relative isolation, Vanuatu has had a significant impact on global efforts to protect and preserve the natural world.

**C** However, the country's commitment to conservation was on full display after this, as Vanuatu worked to rebuild and restore its natural and cultural assets.

**D** As a result, Vanuatu has been a leading voice in global efforts to reduce greenhouse gas emissions and promote adaptation measures to help communities cope with the impacts of climate change.

**E** Plant life thrives in Vanuatu due to lots of rain, the right soil and twelve months of humidity.

**F** In addition to its cultural conservation efforts, Vanuatu has also been at the front of marine conservation.

**G** This includes initiatives such as ecotourism, cultural tourism and community-based tourism, which can help to generate income for local communities while also promoting conservation and cultural preservation.

# Part 8

You are going to read in which five people talk about their experiences of working from home during the Covid-19 pandemic. For questions 47–56, select the correct paragraph (A–E). Each paragraph may be selected more than once.

**Which person:**

| | |
|---|---|
| learned new strategies during the pandemic and wants to use them in their new schedule? | **47** |
| learned that positivity and determination can help beat the most difficult challenges in life? | **48** |
| likes that that they didn't waste time travelling to and from work? | **49** |
| was initially a little anxious with regard to how they would cope with working from home? | **50** |
| felt very happy when the pandemic ended? | **51** |
| experienced little to no change? | **52** |
| found it difficult at first to get used to the technology but figured it out in the end? | **53** |
| found staying inside quite lonely due to a lack of physical contact with colleagues? | **54** |
| was constantly distracted by family members? | **55** |
| felt sad for those who were not used to working from home? | **56** |

# Working from home during the Covid-19 pandemic

**A**

When the pandemic hit, my job moved online and, at first, I was nervous about how I would adapt to working from home. It was all a big rush. As time went on, I began to embrace the change and have never looked back since. One of the things I enjoy about working from home is the flexibility it offers. Additionally, I no longer have to worry about the daily commute, which saves me both time and money. To make the change to working from home smoother, I had to get organised and establish a routine. I found that using technology, such as video-conferencing software, helped me to stay connected with my colleagues and maintain a sense of community, despite not physically being in the same office.

**B**

As a freelancer, I have worked from home throughout most of my career, so the pandemic did not bring any significant changes to my work routine. Whilst others were adjusting to the new reality of remote work, I continued with my usual routine and did not find anything particularly special about working from home. As someone who had always been used to setting my own working patterns, keeping clear of distractions during the working day and putting in place a clear boundary between 'work time' and 'home time', I must admit that I occasionally got frustrated with my colleagues' initial troubles. I had little sympathy with complaints of loneliness and people feeling disconnected from their colleagues. However, I did feel sorry for people trying to manage being parents alongside working from home, and of course, I had a lot of sympathy for younger people who were missing out on their social life with friends.

**C**

During the pandemic, I worked from home. I was used to working in an office, surrounded by my colleagues and having all the necessary gadgets. But then everything changed. I had to work remotely, which meant that I had to use a lot of new equipment to stay connected with my colleagues. To be honest, I was never good with technology, so I had to learn a lot of new skills quickly. I had to set up video calls, share screens and collaborate on documents with people in other buildings. It was difficult, but I managed to get the hang of it eventually. On top of all this, I had two young children to look after. They were too young to understand why I had to work from home, so they kept interrupting me during the day. It was incredibly stressful, and I often felt like I wasn't doing anything right. I hated working from home, and I was over the moon when the pandemic was over!

**D**

During lockdown, I moved my work online and was able to achieve a much better work-life balance than ever before. I cut out my daily commute and the stresses that come with it, and I had more time to spend with my family. Working from home meant that I could structure my day in a way that suited me, rather than having to follow a strict office schedule. I'm back in the office a few days a week now, but I still work from home for the rest of the time. While I'm glad to have some face-to-face interaction with my colleagues again, I'm worried that I'll lose the balance I achieved during lockdown. I know that it's possible to have a healthy balance between work and family, even if it takes a little more effort. I'm grateful for the lessons I learned during the pandemic, and I'm confident that I can apply them to my new routine.

**E**

I'm in my 50s and working from home during the Covid-19 pandemic was a significant challenge for me. I found the isolation of remote work difficult, as I am used to working in a physical office environment where I can interact with colleagues and collaborate on projects. The lack of face-to-face communication made it challenging to build relationships and maintain a sense of team spirit. Fortunately, with time I was able to overcome these challenges. I took online courses to improve my technical skills, and I made an effort to contact colleagues more frequently. While remote work remains a challenge for me, I have come to appreciate the flexibility and convenience it provides. I have learned that with a positive attitude, even the most challenging situations can be overcome.

Name _____     Date _____

## Part 5
Mark the appropriate answer (A, B, C or D).     (6 marks)

| 0 | A | B | C■ | D |
|---|---|---|---|---|

| 31 | A | B | C | D | | 34 | A | B | C | D |
|---|---|---|---|---|---|---|---|---|---|---|
| 32 | A | B | C | D | | 35 | A | B | C | D |
| 33 | A | B | C | D | | 36 | A | B | C | D |

## Part 6
Add the appropriate answer (A–D).     (4 marks)

| 37 | 38 | 39 | 40 |
|---|---|---|---|

## Part 7
Add the appropriate answer (A–G).     (6 marks)

| 41 | 42 | 43 |
|---|---|---|
| 44 | 45 | 46 |

## Part 8
Add the appropriate answer (A–E).     (10 marks)

| 47 | 48 | 49 | 50 | 51 |
|---|---|---|---|---|
| 52 | 53 | 54 | 55 | 56 |

# Cambridge
# C1 Advanced
# Reading

# Test 6

# Part 5

You are going to read an extract from an interview in which a man named Dr. Steven Gibbons talks about melatonin – a chemical in the body. For questions 31–36, mark the appropriate answer (A, B, C or D) that you think fits best according to the text.

## Melatonin

Today, Dr. Steven Gibbons discusses the chemical properties of the melatonin hormone, which is a natural chemical in our bodies, and the health implications associated with its use.

"Melatonin is a hormone that is produced naturally by the body and plays an essential role in regulating the 'sleep-wake cycle'. It primarily comes from a place deep within the brain. Melatonin is primarily responsible for regulating body rhythms and promoting sleep. It has also been linked to several health benefits, which I'll discuss later in more detail.

The chemical properties of melatonin are quite unique. Firstly, they are structurally similar to the hormone that influences happiness, memory and learning, among other things. Melatonin and serotonin produce a reaction when they come together. This happens through a two-step process. The first step involves converting the serotonin hormone which is then converted to melatonin. Melatonin is then able to cross the blood-brain barrier and enter the brain.

The production of melatonin is regulated by the body's internal clock, which is influenced by external things such as light and temperature. Melatonin increases when its dark, and decreases when its light, therefore Melatonin levels in the body are highest at night and lowest during the day. This is why melatonin is often referred to as the 'hormone of darkness'. Melatonin signals to the body that it is time to close your eyes and helps to promote the beginning of sleep.

In addition to its role in regulating the sleep-wake cycle, melatonin has been linked to several other health benefits, such as fighting infections, reducing anxiety and depression, and improving how the blood moves around your body. In general, a person's body produces enough melatonin for its general needs. However, some studies show that melatonin tablets help promote sleep and are suitable for short-term use, if a person is struggling with insomnia, or a lack of sleep. Melatonin tablets have become increasingly popular in recent years, particularly as a sleep aid. By 2021 its production had become a billion-dollar, global business, with demand nowadays continuing to expand.

However, too much melatonin can make a person feel tired during the day. This can make it difficult to concentrate or perform daily activities. Some people become dizzy after taking melatonin, which can be especially dangerous when driving or operating machinery. Headaches are also common and can be particularly painful. Then we have upset stomachs and sickness, often resulting in a visit to the toilet. Strangely, melatonin can also cause sleep disturbances in some people. This can involve vivid dreams, nightmares and sleepwalking, along with severe anxiety. However, research is yet to be carried out on the reasons why this sometimes occurs.

Despite these concerns, melatonin tablets can be effective for some people. They may be particularly helpful for individuals who have trouble falling asleep or staying asleep, such as those who have travelled long distances or people who work long hours. But remember, it is important to follow the recommended dose and to use melatonin tablets only for short periods of time. It is not advised that you take them over a long period."

**31**  In the first paragraph, the writer emphasises how melatonin

   **A**  is a natural chemical.

   **B**  influences our hormones.

   **C**  affects our body and well-being.

   **D**  is good for our health.

**32**  The writer explains that melatonin

   **A**  hides within the brain.

   **B**  produces regular hormones.

   **C**  makes our bodies stronger.

   **D**  helps regulate our body clocks.

**33**  The writer says that a person's body patterns are affected by

   **A**  outside signals like temperature and daylight.

   **B**  the beginning and continuing of sleep.

   **C**  low temperatures late at night.

   **D**  shutting your eyes and going to sleep.

**34**  What does the writer say about the growth of the melatonin tablet trade?

   **A**  It will only get bigger.

   **B**  It will become an international business.

   **C**  It is becoming dangerous.

   **D**  It will become a part of our everyday lives.

**35**  In paragraph 6, why does the writer use 'strangely' to talk about melatonin?

   **A**  because it is supposed to help a person sleep

   **B**  because there isn't much research on the subject

   **C**  because it can make a person feel tired during the day

   **D**  because it gives a person anxiety

**36**  The writer says that taking melatonin tablets is not suitable

   **A**  for a short-term problem.

   **B**  for those who work late nights.

   **C**  for people who want to travel.

   **D**  for a large amount of time.

# Part 6

**You are going to read four opinions about being in a band. For questions 37–40, choose from the opinions A–D. The opinions may be selected more than once.**

## Being in a band

### A – Sonia

I'm a professional musician, and I take music pretty seriously. However, it is something that was born out of the love and enjoyment of music, so it never feels like hard work. I have been playing music for over twenty years and have been in numerous bands throughout my career. When I was younger, I found it difficult sometimes to express myself in rehearsals and, to be honest, I think I was probably quite bossy. I had many silly arguments with bandmates. But over the years I have got better at listening to others and being a team-player. Playing music with others is like having a conversation. Each musician brings their own ideas and perspectives, and together we create something that is greater than most things in this world. I value that above everything else nowadays.

### B – Charles

I've been playing guitar for 10 years, so I've been in a few bands, but the one I'm in now is definitely the best. I'm at college studying chemistry, but we manage to rehearse at least once a week and play live now and again. It's not how I earn a living, but I do consider myself to be an accomplished amateur. I love the challenge of learning new songs and working together to create a strong performance. There's something special about playing music with other people. You develop a bond that is hard to explain. We all understand each other, and nothing else matters. The feeling of going on stage though is the best part of it for me. Playing in front of people can be scary, but there is nothing to compare to the sound of the audience cheering when you get on stage or finish a great song.

### C – Emily

I'm a high school student and I took up the guitar about two years ago. The music teacher in school encouraged me to join a group with some other students from my year. I was nervous at first, but after we managed to play our first few songs I was fine. I realised that everyone was just doing their best. In our band, all the girls are really cool. We usually choose songs by famous artists to sing, but we have said that we'd like to write our own songs in the future. Mark, our music teacher, said that if we want to we can play in the end-of-year show in June. That's a bit scary at the moment, but we'll see how we feel about it closer to the time. These are people who understand me and share my love for music. It's an incredible feeling to be part of something like this.

### D – Jakob

I am a software engineer during the day and a drummer at night. I've been playing since I was about 10 and I'm quite decent now. For me, being in a band is all about the performance. I love the thrill of playing live in front of an audience. Playing music is great, but there's something extra special about playing live. It's like you're giving a piece of yourself to the audience, and they're giving back to you. There's nothing quite like it. I've been in the same band for four years. To be honest, I don't really get on with the singer. He's selfish and I can't be bothered with him. I'm good mates with the other guys though, but bands can be a bit like that. You sometimes get on with other band members better than others, and that has an impact when you make decisions about what direction the band is taking. Anyway – I just love playing.

**Which person:**

has a different experience in terms of time in the music business comparec to the others?

| 37 | |

shares a similar opinion with D about playing live?

| 38 | |

shares A's negative experiences with bandmates?

| 39 | |

expresses the same opinion as B about creating music as a whole?

| 40 | |

# Part 7

You are going to read an extract from a newspaper article about Lawrence of Arabia. Six paragraphs have been removed. Select from the paragraphs A–G the one that fits each gap (questions 41–46). There is one extra paragraph that you do not need to use.

## Lawrence of Arabia

T.E. Lawrence, also known as Lawrence of Arabia, was a British officer, diplomat and writer who played a significant role in the Arab Revolt against the Ottoman Empire during World War I.

Lawrence was born on August 16, 1888, in Tremadog, Wales, and grew up in Oxford, England.

| 41 | |
|---|---|

After graduation, Lawrence worked as an archaeologist in the Middle East, which is where he developed an interest in Arab culture and politics.

In 1914, Lawrence was recruited as a spy by the British Army's Intelligence Department to serve in the Middle East. He was told to get information on the Ottoman Empire, which was an ally of Germany during World War I. Lawrence quickly proved himself to be very skilled, using his knowledge of Arabic and his understanding of Arab culture to gather valuable information.

| 42 | |
|---|---|

He quickly became a close ally of the Arab leader, Prince Faisal, and played a key role in organising and leading his army.

Lawrence was known for surprising the enemy, which caused significant damage to Ottoman infrastructure. His most famous attack was on the Ottoman-held city of Aqaba, which was considered impossible to take over due to its location and defences. The capture of Aqaba was a significant turning point in the Arab Revolt, and Lawrence became a hero in both Arab and British circles. His efforts were crucial in getting the support of the Arab tribes and appearing united against the Ottomans.

Despite his successes, Lawrence was not without his criticisms.

| 43 | |
|---|---|

Lawrence was also accused of exaggerating his achievements.

After the end of World War I, Lawrence became a supporter of Arab independence and worked very hard to promote the Arab cause. He was heavily involved in negotiating the Arab-British Treaty of 1922, which recognised the independence of several Arab states and established British influence in the region.

| 44 | |
|---|---|

In 1926, Lawrence retired from the military and began a new career as a writer. He wrote several books, including *Seven Pillars of Wisdom*, which told of his experiences during the Arab Revolt.

| 45 | |
|---|---|

Lawrence remained a controversial figure throughout his life. He was admired by some as a hero who fought for Arab independence, while others saw him as an adventurer who didn't always tell the truth. Despite the controversies, Lawrence is often thought of as a charming and brave leader who fought for a just cause. Lawrence's story extends far beyond the Arab Revolt, however. His ideas and actions continue to influence the region and the world to this day. His support for Arab independence and his understanding of the importance of cultural sensitivity in diplomacy and military operations are still relevant in today's complex political landscape. Lawrence died on May 19, 1935, at the age of 46, in a motorcycle accident.

| 46 | |
|---|---|

However, the man's influence lives on, and his story continues to inspire generations of people around the world.

**A** However, Lawrence's true usefulness became clear when he was sent to Arabia to work with the Arab Revolt against the Ottoman Empire.

**B** Some British officers saw him as someone who operated alone and did not follow traditional military tactics.

**C** However, he was disappointed with the final outcome of the agreement, feeling that the Arab people had not been given the independence they deserved.

**D** Although his life was represented in the historical film *Lawrence of Arabia*, directed by David Lean and starring Peter O'Toole as Lawrence himself.

**E** It became a bestseller and is still considered one of the greatest personal books of the 20th century

**F** Lawrence was an exceptional student and received a scholarship to study at Jesus College in the UK, where he did very well in medieval history and archaeology.

**G** It was a shock to his family, friends and admirers all over the world.

# Part 8

**You are going to read a newspaper article in which five archaeologists talk about their most interesting discovery. For questions 47–56, select the correct paragraph (A–E). Each paragraph may be selected more than once.**

**Which person:**

| | |
|---|---|
| found something that presented information on methods of production in the past? | 47 |
| discovered something to help the authorities solve a case? | 48 |
| found something that may have attracted people from other places? | 49 |
| reshaped the historical relationships between two countries? | 50 |
| contributed to research in many different countries and is included in educational papers? | 51 |
| graduated recently and is happy to work? | 52 |
| found something unexpectedly due to construction work? | 53 |
| discovered that humans occupied the area prior to what was initially believed? | 54 |
| was in charge of the project? | 55 |
| talks about how much we still don't know? | 56 |

# My best ever archaeological discovery

**A**

I've spent countless hours digging and studying ancient objects, but this discovery was unlike any other. I was leading a team in a remote area of Scotland, searching for evidence of an early Celtic community. We weren't expecting to find anything Roman, as the empire's influence in Scotland was thought to be minimal, but, as I was carefully brushing away the dirt one morning, I saw it – a small Roman coin. As we continued to dig, we uncovered more and more Roman items – a statue, military clothing and beautifully preserved glass. It was an incredible discovery, one that would rewrite the history of Scotland's relationship with the Roman Empire. Discovering something like this was the most amazing time of my career. It's why I love what I do – and I feel incredibly fortunate to have been a part of it.

**B**

As an industrial archaeologist, I've had the privilege of working on many fascinating projects throughout my career, but one discovery stands out above all the rest. While conducting a survey of an abandoned factory in the mid-western United States, my team and I found a hidden room by accident. Inside the room, we found a treasure of machinery and equipment that had been used in the factory's early days. As we continued to explore, we found a plan that detailed the factory's original design and construction. This was an incredible find, as it gave us a glimpse into the past and showed how the factory had evolved over time. It also had significant historical value, as it provided insights into the manufacturing processes of the time and the technologies that were used. The find showed the importance of industrial archaeology and the value of preserving these sites for future generations.

**C**

While conducting surveys in the region, we noticed an unusual pattern of vegetation growth in a remote area. With further investigation, we uncovered the remains of a previously unknown city, hidden for centuries beneath the thick jungle. The discovery of the lost city has the potential to modify our understanding of ancient civilisations in the region. The project has already shown significant insights into ancient South American societies. Our work will be published in academic journals and shared with scholars around the world, contributing to our collective understanding of the region's history.

**D**

I have been working in collaboration with the local police department on a recent project in the area of a suspected criminal activity site. During the course of the project, I made an interesting discovery, uncovering a number of items that seem to be linked to a previous civilisation that inhabited the area. The items include pottery, stone tools and animal bones. This is of great significance, if true, as it suggests that the area was inhabited by humans much earlier than previously thought. It has also been suggested that the items may be relevant to what happened, as they could indicate a possible motive for the criminal activity in the area. I am confident that the work will be of great value to the police.

**E**

As a newly qualified archaeologist fresh out of education, I was thrilled to be part of a team that discovered a Roman temple in a field that was scheduled to have a road built through it. The temple was an unexpected discovery, as the area had not been previously identified as having any significant archaeological remains. The structure was surprisingly new, with many of the original sub-structures and objects still in place. It was an exciting time for us, as we uncovered many fascinating items such as pottery, jewellery and coins. The temple itself is an impressive structure. We believe that it would have been a place of worship for the local Roman population, and perhaps even a place for other people to visit from other parts of the empire.

Name  _____          Date  _____

## Part 5
Mark the appropriate answer (A, B, C or D).          (6 marks)

| 0 | A | B | C | D |
|---|---|---|---|---|

| 31 | A | B | C | D | | 34 | A | B | C | D |
|----|---|---|---|---|---|----|---|---|---|---|
| 32 | A | B | C | D | | 35 | A | B | C | D |
| 33 | A | B | C | D | | 36 | A | B | C | D |

## Part 6
Add the appropriate answer (A–D).          (4 marks)

| 37 | 38 | 39 | 40 |
|----|----|----|----|

## Part 7
Add the appropriate answer (A–G).          (6 marks)

| 41 | 42 | 43 |
|----|----|----|
| 44 | 45 | 46 |

## Part 8
Add the appropriate answer (A–E).          (10 marks)

| 47 | 48 | 49 | 50 | 51 |
|----|----|----|----|----|
| 52 | 53 | 54 | 55 | 56 |

# Cambridge
# C1 Advanced
# Reading

# Test 7

## Part 5

**You are going to read an extract from a newspaper article about how to get a job in Artificial Intelligence (AI). For questions 31–36, mark the appropriate answer (A, B, C or D) that you think fits best according to the text.**

## How to get a job in Artificial Intelligence (AI)

As the use of Artificial Intelligence (AI) continues to grow, it has become a concern for many industries regarding the impact it may have on employment. For example, jobs such as data entry, administrative tasks and manual labour may be replaced by AI systems that can perform these tasks faster and more efficiently. Other industries, such as manufacturing and transportation, may also see significant changes as AI becomes more common. However, it is important to note that while some jobs may be lost, new opportunities for employment may also arise as a result of the growth of AI, particularly in fields such as data analysis and programming. It is therefore essential for individuals and organisations to adapt and develop new skills in order to stay relevant and competitive in the changing job market.

So, what kind of jobs should young people be considering if they want to work in AI? Most current jobs use AI to focus on a limited set of tasks. Young people who are interested in working with AI in this category should consider pursuing careers in areas such as data science, machine learning and computer programming. These jobs require a high level of technical understanding, and are in high demand in workplaces such as hospitals and banking. As technology continues to evolve and expand, new job opportunities are emerging in a variety of fields, such as researching and creating AI that can think and make choices, so that may be something to look for in the future.

Data science is a field that is rapidly growing in popularity, as businesses look to extract valuable insights from vast amounts of data. Data scientists are responsible for collecting, analysing and interpreting complex data sets. Machine learning is another field that is in high demand. Machine-learning engineers work to develop data that can learn and adapt to new data, helping to improve the accuracy and efficiency of AI systems. Finally, computer programming is a skill that is essential for working with AI technology. Programmers are responsible for developing and maintaining the software and algorithms that power AI systems.

Sarah is an example of a young person who has followed the route of technology. She is a recent graduate who has just started her first job in the field. Sarah always had an interest in technology, and really enjoyed finding solutions to puzzles and technical dilemmas throughout school, which led her to pursue a degree in computer science. During her studies, she developed a particular interest in machine learning and AI, and she sought out opportunities to gain hands-on experience in these areas.

After completing her degree, Sarah managed to get a job as a data scientist at a healthcare technology company in Silicon Valley. AI has the potential to help the healthcare industry in numerous ways, from improving patient outcomes to enhancing administrative jobs. Sarah is responsible for developing models that can help patients. She works closely with physicians and data analysts to identify key data, and then uses machine-learning data to extract insights and build such models.

Despite being new to the field, Sarah has quickly become an integral member of the team. She helps them learn just as much as they learn themselves. She has demonstrated a love for her job, a willingness to learn and a passion for using AI to make a positive impact on the healthcare industry. She is also doing as much professional development as possible, attending conferences and workshops to stay up to date on the latest trends in AI. Her dream is to move into a leadership role where she can be part of the future of technology.

As with any employment, it's important to research the areas you're interested in, the jobs that are available and the skills they require. Work in AI often requires studies in computer science, coding and maths, so check which universities offer those courses. Once you're at university, see which areas of AI you enjoy the most and look for opportunities for further studies, training or work. Make connections with people in the field and always show how keen you are. AI and technology are moving very fast, so always check what's new and maybe one day, you'll be the one behind it!

**31** While AI could take over a number of jobs, it is also important to see that

    **A**    administrative tasks and manual labour may undergo big changes.

    **B**    there may be significant job loss in data analysis and programming.

    **C**    there may be many more new job opportunities.

    **D**    manufacturing and transportation may be irreplaceable.

**32** In paragraph 2 the writer mentions three fields that demand

    **A**    a strong awareness of technical knowledge.

    **B**    knowledge of healthcare and finance.

    **C**    thinking and decision-making skills.

    **D**    growth and evolution across different areas.

**33** What does the writer say about businesses that use data science?

    **A**    They are keen on extracting information from data scientists.

    **B**    They are becoming solely focused on data science.

    **C**    They are growing day by day.

    **D**    They are interested in gaining knowledge from the data available.

**34** What made Sarah want to study computer science?

    **A**    She had always been interested in machines.

    **B**    She loved solving problems as a child.

    **C**    She already had experience in machine learning.

    **D**    She wanted to be a data scientist.

**35** In the sixth paragraph, what is Sarah's goal?

    **A**    To manage others and create new technology.

    **B**    To be known for her enthusiasm and skills.

    **C**    To run training sessions for other teams.

    **D**    To teach other members of her team.

**36** In the final paragraph, what advice does the writer give once you start studying?

    **A**    Try to get employed as fast as possible.

    **B**    Take on any available job to show how eager you are.

    **C**    Figure out what you like and find experience within that field.

    **D**    Research all available courses.

# Part 6

You are going to read four reviews about Geoffrey Holland's crime novel *The Black Apple*. For questions 37–40, choose from the reviews A–D. The reviews may be selected more than once.

## The Black Apple

### A

*The Black Apple* by Geoffrey Holland is a crime fiction novel set in New York in the early 1950s. The plot is about a series of crimes, including a series of horrible murders and a communist investigation by the New York Police Department (NYPD). The main character is Ivan Smalley, a young and ambitious detective who becomes involved in the case when he discovers a link between the murders and a movie studio where he works part-time. The plot of the book is heavy and detailed, with numerous sub-plots and multiple perspectives. It is a dark representation of New York in the 1950s, with themes of corruption, power and violence, which some may find a bit much. Holland's writing style is quick, with a focus on dialogue and distinctive use of words. Overall, *The Black Apple* is a gripping and powerful read and a worthy addition to the genre of crime fiction – if you like that sort of thing!

### B

*The Black Apple* by Geoffrey Holland is full of dark language. He uses a unique blend of slang, bad words and street talk to create a vivid world that takes the reader into 1950s New York. His use of language is so effective that you can almost smell the smoke-filled bars, feel the heat of the neon lights and taste the bitterness of the whiskey. Holland is a master of dialogue, and his characters speak in a way that is both authentic and fascinating. The dialogue is filled with energy, and as you read you can almost hear the real-life conversations. The language used in *The Black Apple* is not easy to read though. Holland likes to use bad language and includes descriptions of violence and sex. However, his use of bad language is there for a reason, and every word is carefully chosen to create a specific effect. The writing is dark, but it is also poetic and beautiful in its own way.

### C

Raymond Chandler and Dashiell Hammett, two of the most famous authors of this genre, can be seen throughout *The Black Apple* in terms of writing style. The novel's setting, New York in the 1950s, also reflects the influence of these earlier authors, as this was a popular location for many of their stories. Overall, I like Holland's writing but sometimes it can be a bit too dark for me. Thankfully, Holland's writing style is not only limited to the crime fiction genre. Faulkner's use of multiple characters and indirect storytelling can also be seen in *The Black Apple*, where the story is told from the perspectives of several different characters, each with their own unique voice and point of view. Holland is definitely on the same level as both Chandler and Hammett, and his books are wonderful assets to the crime genre as a whole.

### D

As a reader of crime fiction, I was eager to read Geoffrey Holland's *The Black Apple*. Holland's use of the detective genre to promote his political opinions was far too obvious, and it stopped me from enjoying the book. The novel's plot is centered around the investigation of a series of brutal murders in 1950s New York, but the story is constantly interrupted by Holland's heavy commentary on politics and society. It feels like he is trying to show his own political opinions rather than simply tell an interesting story. It is also clear that he has been influenced by other crime genre authors. In fact, almost too much. Overall, I found *The Black Apple* to be a disappointing read. If you're looking for a crime novel with a strong political message, this book may be for you, but if you prefer your crime fiction to be more focused on the story and characters, you may want to avoid this one.

**Which person:**

expresses the same opinion as B on the specific choice of language?    | 37 |   |

differs from the others regarding the overall opinion of the book?    | 38 |   |

shares a similar view to C regarding the significance of the book?    | 39 |   |

expresses the same opinion as D on the impact of other crime writers?    | 40 |   |

# Part 7

**You are going to read an extract from a newspaper article about public healthcare. Six paragraphs have been removed. Select from the paragraphs A–G the one that fits each gap (questions 41–46). There is one extra paragraph that you do not need to use.**

## Public Healthcare

Public healthcare systems are the foundation of modern societies. They ensure that every citizen, regardless of their income or social status, has access to healthcare services when they need them.

| 41 | |
|---|---|

One of the main arguments for public healthcare systems is the principle of equality. A public system ensures that everyone has access to the same standard of care, regardless of their financial situation. This means that poor and working-class citizens are not left behind, and that they can receive adequate medical attention just as the wealthy do.

| 42 | |
|---|---|

While the government provides healthcare coverage for certain groups, such as the elderly and those on low incomes, the majority of Americans are covered by private insurance plans or pay for healthcare themselves.

| 43 | |
|---|---|

Despite these efforts, however, the United States has yet to implement a public healthcare system at the national level.

The Covid-19 pandemic provides a perfect example of why a public healthcare system is essential. In countries such as the United Kingdom, where the National Health Service (NHS) is the public healthcare system, medical staff worked very hard to save the lives of those affected by the virus. The NHS was able to provide free testing, hospitalisation and treatment for all Covid-19 patients, regardless of their financial situation.

| 44 | |
|---|---|

Another crucial argument for public healthcare systems is how they are able to prevent many diseases before they occur.

This is achieved through measures such as vaccinations and health education programs.

A public system has the capacity to identify and manage potential health risks, which ultimately reduces the burden on the healthcare system as a whole. One example of a public healthcare campaign aimed at reducing alcohol consumption comes from Scotland's national health service. The campaign, called 'Count 14', wants to reduce the number of alcohol units consumed by adults to 14 or fewer per week.

| 45 | |
|---|---|

The campaign also includes a digital unit calculator that allows people to easily calculate how many units of alcohol they are consuming. Additionally, the campaign works with local communities to create alcohol-free events and activities, as well as provide support for those struggling with alcohol addiction. The Count 14 campaign has been successful in raising awareness of the risks associated with excessive alcohol consumption and has led to a reduction in the number of units of alcohol consumed by adults in Scotland.

The campaign's success was due to its comprehensive approach, which includes education, support and community involvement. By providing information and resources to help people make informed decisions about their alcohol consumption, the campaign has helped individuals to take control of their health and well-being. In conclusion, public healthcare systems are vital to ensure that all citizens have access to the best healthcare possible, regardless of their financial status.

| 46 | |
|---|---|

The provision of healthcare is not a privilege but a basic right that should be accessible to everyone.

**A** Despite this, public healthcare systems have been under attack in recent years, with some countries opting for privatised healthcare. This is a dangerous trend that threatens the well-being of millions of people, and it must be stopped.

**B** To ensure that everyone receives the healthcare they need, the current attacks on public healthcare must be stopped. The Covid-19 pandemic has shown that public healthcare systems are the most effective in times of crisis, and they are also the most effective at helping to prevent certain illnesses and diseases.

**C** Contrast this with the US, where people had to pay for Covid-19 testing and treatment. This meant that many people who could not afford it were left untreated, putting themselves and others at risk.

**D** In contrast, a private system would result in only those who can afford it receiving the best care, while the rest of the population is left to suffer. The United States mostly has a private healthcare system, with a mix of private and public insurance programmes.

**E** Groups here have been active in supporting public healthcare, including labour unions, consumer groups and progressive political organisations. In recent years, the issue has gained more attention as the cost of healthcare in the United States continues to rise and the number of uninsured Americans remains high.

**F** It uses a variety of media, including television, radio and social media, to encourage people to drink more responsibly. The campaign's slogan also emphasises the health benefits of reducing alcohol consumption.

**G** The United Kingdom's healthcare service, which was created under Clement Atlee's Labour government in 1948, aimed to provide free healthcare to those who needed it. The costs would be covered by the taxes people pay, which are based on people's annual income.

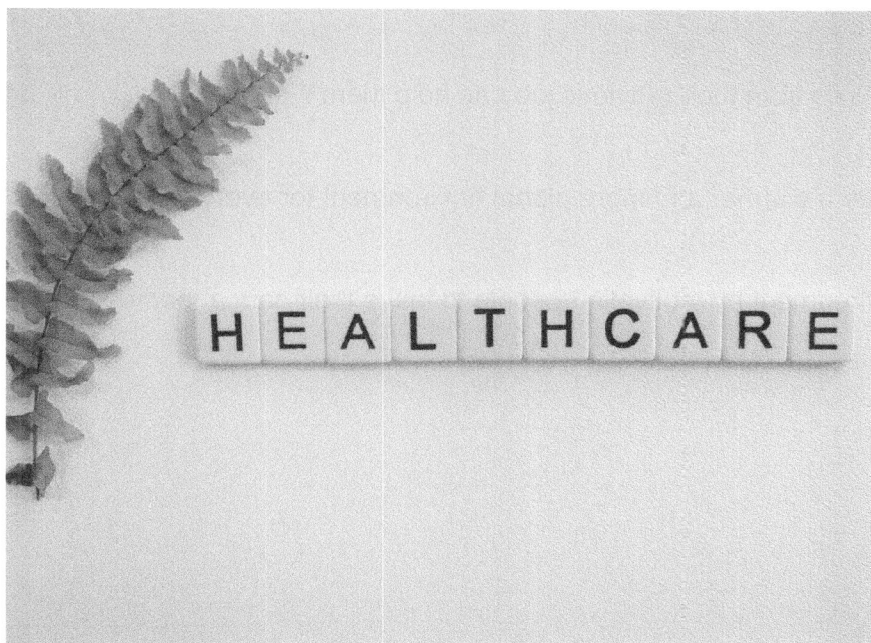

# Part 8

You are going to read a newspaper article in which five young politicians present their plans. For questions 47–56, select the correct paragraph (A–E). Each paragraph may be selected more than once.

**Which person:**

| | |
|---|---|
| says they worked in a school before competing in the local election? | **47** |
| focuses on the development of transportation? | **48** |
| explains how they participate in local campaigns related to the environment? | **49** |
| aims to make the centre of town enjoyable for everybody? | **50** |
| improves infrastructure for those with issues moving around freely? | **51** |
| describes how they help with the reduction of air pollution? | **52** |
| says that increasing employment will lead to an improvement in the economy? | **53** |
| believes the skills from their previous job can help them if elected? | **54** |
| wants to create a warmer and more global environment for everybody? | **55** |
| helps the environment by motivating people to leave their cars at home? | **56** |

# Vote for me, vote green

**A**

I strongly believe that I am the best candidate to represent the green issues in our community. Over the years, I have been actively involved in various environmental campaigns and initiatives aimed at creating a cleaner, greener and sustainable future for our town. If elected at the next local election, I promise to continue fighting for green initiatives that will help reduce the effects of climate change and protect our environment. In the past, I was involved with a very successful transport scheme that encouraged people to stop driving and start using public transport. My vision is to work with local businesses, community leaders, teachers and residents to develop practical solutions to reduce our carbon footprint, improve air quality and ensure that our environment remains healthy for future generations. Therefore, I ask for your vote so that together we can build a cleaner and greener future for our town.

**B**

I believe that it is time for a change in the way we think about our town. We need to renew our town centre to make it more modern and attractive to visitors and residents alike. I have a bold vision that involves improving public spaces and providing better things to do. This will encourage more people to come into town and enjoy the unique shops, restaurants and entertainment that we have to offer. I also want to improve education and open more schools with more choice for young people. My goal is to make our town centre the heart of our community, a place where people can come together to shop, dine and socialise. I urge you to vote for me in the upcoming election so that we can work together to create a town centre that we can all be proud of.

**C**

I want to highlight the issue of accessibility at our town's train station. Currently, our station is not fully accessible for people with disabilities, particularly those who use wheelchairs. As a politician, I believe it is my duty to work towards making our town more accessible for everyone. If elected, I will prioritise the issue of accessibility at our town's station by working with local authorities, disability rights groups and the wider community to develop a plan that will make our station fully wheelchair accessible. By doing this, we can create a welcoming and inclusive environment for all and ensure that everyone has the opportunity to travel by train, regardless of their mobility needs. I encourage you to vote for me so that we can come together to make our community a place where everyone can thrive and feel valued.

**D**

As a retired headmaster and a lifelong resident of this community, you should vote for me in the upcoming local election. I believe that my experience in education and my commitment to the improvement of our community makes me uniquely qualified to lead. During my years as an educator, I learned how to balance budgets, manage personnel and work collaboratively with diverse groups. I have also noticed the changes in attitude towards the environment and climate change, especially with young people. Their skills and experiences can be applied to the challenges facing our community today. I am committed to ensuring that our community is safe, prosperous and an enjoyable place to live. I believe that my leadership, experience and commitment to this community make me the best candidate for the job.

**E**

I am passionate about our town and its potential for growth and development. If elected, I will develop a comprehensive plan to attract new businesses to our town, which will generate more revenue and create jobs. This will involve working with local entrepreneurs, community leaders and investors to identify opportunities and promote our town's strengths and unique selling points. I will also work to improve the infrastructure in our town, such as train links, high-speed internet and public services, which will make our town more attractive to investors. By doing so, we can encourage more businesses to open in our town, which will create economic growth and prosperity that will benefit us all. By working together, we can create a brighter future for our town.

Name  _____       Date  _____

## Part 5

Mark the appropriate answer (A, B, C or D).                              (6 marks)

| 0 | A | B | C | D | |
|---|---|---|---|---|---|

| 31 | A | B | C | D | |  | 34 | A | B | C | D | |
|----|---|---|---|---|---|--|----|---|---|---|---|---|
| 32 | A | B | C | D | |  | 35 | A | B | C | D | |
| 33 | A | B | C | D | |  | 36 | A | B | C | D | |

## Part 6

Add the appropriate answer (A–D).                                       (4 marks)

| 37 | | 38 | | 39 | | 40 | |
|----|--|----|--|----|--|----|--|

## Part 7

Add the appropriate answer (A–G).                                       (6 marks)

| 41 | | 42 | | 43 | |
|----|--|----|--|----|--|
| 44 | | 45 | | 46 | |

## Part 8

Add the appropriate answer (A–E).                                       (10 marks)

| 47 | | 48 | | 49 | | 50 | | 51 | |
|----|--|----|--|----|--|----|--|----|--|
| 52 | | 53 | | 54 | | 55 | | 56 | |

# Cambridge
# C1 Advanced
# Reading

# Test 8

## Part 5

**You are going to read an extract from a newspaper article about a day in the life of a barista – someone who makes coffee for a living. For questions 31–36, mark the appropriate answer (A, B, C or D) that you think fits best according to the text.**

## A day in the life of a barista

Being a barista is more than just making coffee. It is an art form that requires a unique combination of skills, knowledge and passion. A day in the life of a barista is a busy and rewarding experience, and is full of challenges and opportunities.

The day usually starts early, as coffee shops are busiest in the morning when people are on their way to work or starting their day. As a result, baristas need to be ready to serve customers as soon as the shop opens. The barista arrives at work and immediately begins to set up the coffee shop. This involves checking the number of coffee beans, milk and other ingredients, as well as making sure the espresso machine and other equipment are all working.

Once everything is set up, the barista greets customers and takes their orders. This is where the art of being a barista starts. A good barista needs to be knowledgeable about the different types of coffee beans, brewing techniques and flavour profiles. They also need to be able to listen to the customers' preferences and make recommendations based on their tastes.

Next comes the preparation of the coffee. The barista takes the beans and prepares the espresso, carefully measuring the coffee and water to ensure the perfect balance of flavour and strength. They then steam the milk to the correct temperature and texture, creating the silky 'microfoam' that is essential for 'latte art'. Many baristas learn about different coffee-making methods.

As they create the coffee, the barista also talks with customers, answering their questions and making small talk. This is a key part of the job, as it helps to create a welcoming atmosphere in the coffee shop. And don't forget: in the service industry, tips are often an important source of income. A friendly barista who provides excellent customer service is more likely to receive tips, which can help to increase their overall earnings.

Once the coffee is ready, the barista carefully pours it into the cup and adds any requested flavourings. They then use their skills to create 'latte art', which involves pouring steamed milk into espresso to create interesting patterns. This can be a great way to add character to a coffee and impress customers.

Throughout the day, the barista must maintain the coffee shop, ensuring that it remains clean and well-stocked to satisfy all customers' orders. This is essential for several reasons. Firstly, it helps to maintain the quality and taste of the coffee. A dirty shop can lead to a build-up of oils, coffee grounds and excess milk, which can affect the flavour of the coffee. This can be particularly noticeable in drinks where the taste of the coffee is stronger. Secondly, a clean shop helps to prevent food-safety issues. Coffee is a food product after all, and, like all food products, it needs to be prepared and served in a clean and hygienic environment. A dirty shop can be a breeding ground for bacteria, which can cause illness if not properly controlled.

As the day progresses, the barista may also be called upon to prepare food items such as sandwiches or pastries. They must be able to work quickly and efficiently, ensuring that all orders are delivered promptly. In addition to their main duties, a barista also needs to be able to multitask and adapt to changing situations. They may be asked to cover shifts at short notice or deal with unexpected busy periods, for instance. This requires a calm and professional approach, as well as the ability to work under pressure. At the end of the day, the barista cleans and tidies the coffee station, ensuring that it is ready for the next morning. Overall, being a barista is a challenging and rewarding job. It is an art form and an opportunity to create delicious and beautiful coffee that brings joy to customers every day.

**31**   What two things does the writer highlight as being necessary for a barista?

    **A**   To be informed and have a love for the subject.

    **B**   To understand that there are difficulties but also chances involved.

    **C**   To make sure that you are doing things and are challenged.

    **D**   To have experience in coffee making and art.

**32**   Why does the writer highlight the importance of the barista arriving early?

    **A**   The coffee beans need to be counted.

    **B**   All coffee machines need to be checked.

    **C**   There are people who are waiting for the shop to open.

    **D**   There are many potential customers who come in before work.

**33**   Why is it important for a barista to pay attention to their customers?

    **A**   So that they can make the best tasting coffee possible.

    **B**   So that they can advise them on their likes and dislikes.

    **C**   So that they can take their order without any misunderstanding.

    **D**   So that they can learn about making coffee in different ways.

**34**   According to the writer, making small talk is important because

    **A**   it helps the barista know what the customer wants to order.

    **B**   customers often have a lot of questions about their coffee.

    **C**   it helps increase the income of the coffee shop.

    **D**   customers react well to a warm and friendly environment.

**35**   According to the writer, an unclean environment can affect the coffee's

    **A**   stock.

    **B**   taste.

    **C**   oils.

    **D**   preparation.

**36**   What should a barista do when their shift finishes?

    **A**   Make sure that they have made the customers happy.

    **B**   Remain calm and prepare themselves for the next day.

    **C**   Prepare the shop for the following day.

    **D**   Make themselves a delicious coffee.

# Part 6

You are going to read four opinions about being the youngest child in their family. For questions 37–40, choose from the opinions A–D. The opinions may be selected more than once.

## Being the youngest sibling

### A

Being the youngest child in a family can be challenging, especially if you have older brothers or sisters who bully you. Growing up, I often felt like I was being picked on by my brothers, who would tease and exclude me, and make fun of me for things that were out of my control. It was a difficult experience, as it left me feeling insecure and powerless. Bullying can take many forms, from physical violence to verbal abuse. As the youngest, I was particularly at risk to these types of behaviours, as my brothers were bigger and stronger than I was. They knew how to annoy me and make me feel like an outsider in my own family. As I grew physically, I learned to stand up for myself and to state my boundaries with them. Overall, I would prefer to be an only child.

### B

I am four years younger than my next oldest brother, and when I was a kid I was often hidden from the harsh realities of the world. My parents were very protective of me, and my older brother and sisters were encouraged to look out for me and keep me safe. While this had some benefits, such as a sense of security and a close relationship with my siblings, it also had some downsides. I was not allowed to do certain things or go to certain places because my parents thought them too risky or dangerous. While I understood that my parents were trying to protect me, I also felt frustrated and annoyed at times. I relied heavily on my immediate family for support, but this meant that I sometimes struggled to make decisions or take risks on my own.

### C

As a child, I often felt like I could always get my own way. My parents and brothers were always willing to let me get what I wanted, either out of love or anger, and, while this was a nice feeling in some ways it also had some drawbacks. I was used to being catered to, and I didn't always consider the needs or feelings of those around me. It also meant that I needed my parents and brothers' attention to make me feel happy. I was used to getting what I wanted, and when things didn't go my way, I sometimes struggled to cope with the disappointment.

### D

I was often referred to as my mother's favourite when growing up. She loved me and showered me with affection and attention, which made me feel loved and special. However, this also had some negative consequences for my relationship with my sisters who often hated me for the special treatment that I received from our mother. This led to tensions and conflicts between us, and it also made it harder for me to connect with them on a deeper level. Additionally, being my mother's favourite sometimes made me feel guilty or uncomfortable. I knew that my sisters were struggling with their own issues, and that they deserved love and attention as much as I did, and I also worried that this would also create more tension between us that would be hard to mend. I tried to be sensitive to their feelings and to find ways to connect with them. While our family can still be complicated at times, I am grateful for the love and support that we share.

**Which person:**

shares the same experiences as D regarding conflict with siblings?

| 37 | |

has the same view as C regarding being spoilt?

| 38 | |

has a different opinion than the others in terms of having siblings?

| 39 | |

shares a similar view to B about family members altering their mood?

| 40 | |

# Part 7

**You are going to read an extract from a newspaper article about social networks. Six paragraphs have been removed. Select from the paragraphs A–G the one that fits each gap (questions 41–46). There is one extra paragraph that you do not need to use.**

## Are social networks really that social?

In recent years, social media and the internet have altered the way in which we communicate and interact with others. While the internet and social media platforms have made it easier for us to connect with people all over the world, it has been argued that it has led to a decline in our face-to-face interactions, making us less social beings.

**41**

Prior to social media and the internet, people primarily communicated with one another through face-to-face conversations, letters or phone calls. These forms of communication required individuals to invest more time and effort in their interactions, which made them more meaningful and personal.

**42**

We can now easily share updates, photos and messages with our friends and family at the touch of a button, and connect with people instantly and easily, regardless of where they are located in the world. Social media platforms such as Facebook, Twitter and Instagram have produced a new way of communicating with large groups of friends. We may have known some of those people for many years. They may be family, or friends from school or our neighbourhood. They might be what we would consider 'close friends'. They may, however, be people we have met once at a social event and with whom we then decided to swap contact details, therefore 'keeping in contact' in a way that would have been impossible 20 years ago.

Social media and the 'friendships' made through it have created a new way of making friends that must be separated from the traditional idea of being social and having friendships.

**43**

Those who don't achieve these elements of friendship, are considered a failure by others, but more by themselves.

Despite the many advantages that social media and the internet have brought, there is growing concern that our obsession with these technologies is leading to a decline in our social skills and abilities.

**44**

One reason for this is that social media and the internet have made it easier for us to hide behind a screen and avoid in-person interactions. We can now connect with people without having to leave our homes or make any effort to socialise in person. This has led to a decrease in our ability to read and interpret social signals and body language, which are important skills for developing and maintaining relationships.

**45**

However, it is important to note that social media and the internet can also have positive effects. For example, social media can provide a way for individuals to connect with others who share similar interests and experiences, which can help to reduce feelings of loneliness. Furthermore, social media can be a powerful tool for raising awareness about important social and political issues, and for promoting positive social change.

**46**

The impact of social media and the internet on our social lives is complex. It's wonderful to embrace the new tools available to us, but it is also very important to maintain and invest in face-to-face in-person contact.

**A** Research has also shown that people who spend more time on social media are more likely to experience feelings of anxiety, depression and low self-esteem. This can be due to a lack of strong support networks from those we really care about. Furthermore, being outside and getting regular exercise, particularly as part of a group in a team sport, can build a sense of belonging and well-being.

**B** Studies have shown that people who spend more time online and on social media platforms are more likely to experience feelings of loneliness than those who engage in face-to-face interactions.

**C** So, what are the effects that social media and the internet have on our social lives, especially with regard to our mental health and well-being?

**D** Some of the most popular social media platforms in the world will probably change within the next few years due to how fast the digital world is changing.

**E** Through social media, individuals can connect with others who share their beliefs and work together to create positive change in their communities and in society as a whole. Many people have built groups and movements to organise a range of different events, such as cultural, political and environmental ones.

**F** This is because they are different, each with their advantages and disadvantages. One downside of online social networks is that they have created a pressure for users to appear popular, which is determined by the number of photos, comments and 'likes' they receive.

**G** However, with social media and the internet, communication has become much more convenient and accessible. We can use our computers, laptops and phones to contact almost anyone in the world who has access to the internet.

## Part 8

**You are going to read about five hopeful millionaires and their experiences on the TV show 'The Next Big Thing'. For questions 47–56, select the correct paragraph (A–E). Each paragraph may be selected more than once.**

**Which person:**

| | |
|---|---|
| had no clue what to do at the start of the show? | **47** |
| left the show due to personal and moral conflicts? | **48** |
| thought that they were more intelligent than everybody else on the show? | **49** |
| admitted that the whole thing was more difficult than it seemed? | **50** |
| used the skills learnt from the show to create their own company? | **51** |
| did not respect the views and opinions of their teammates? | **52** |
| received terrible feedback from customers? | **53** |
| was not shocked when they were kicked off the show by their teammates? | **54** |
| handled things quite well? | **55** |
| put a lot of money and time into the assignment? | **56** |

# The Next Big Thing

**A**

To be honest, I wasn't surprised when my teammates decided that they wanted me to leave. They were all a bunch of amateurs who couldn't handle my superior intellect and business brain. I tried to work with them, I really did, but they were just so stubborn and narrow-minded. Every time I suggested a new idea, they would say 'no' without even considering it. Of course, they were all just jealous of my success and my natural leadership abilities. They couldn't stand that I was the one in charge, and so they made me leave. They'll see one day that they made a huge mistake by underestimating me.

**B**

I had the worst experience on that show! I thought I could organise a fashion event and make a lot of money, but it turned out to be a total disaster. First, I had no idea what I was doing. I was running around, trying to coordinate everything, but nothing was going according to plan. The worst part was when the whole thing fell apart right in front of the judges. I saw their faces turn from amusement to horror. And when it was all said and done, I got sacked on national television. I was so embarrassed for a while, but then, when the show was on television, I started to get invited onto other shows as a contestant. You know what they say: you live and you learn. And I learned that organising a fashion show is not as easy as it looks!

**C**

Oh dear, that show was a total disaster! I thought I had it all under control – designing a cool new trainer for teenagers would be easy. But I was wrong! The show wanted us to be original, so I was trying to come up with something innovative. I decided that the rest of my team didn't have a clue, so I completely ignored all of their advice. Most of them left me to it, but no matter what I did, I just couldn't get it right. The result was terrible, I hated it. The judges weren't impressed that I had lost the support of my team. I was so caught up in my own ideas that I completely ignored what the teenagers would actually want to wear. You win some, you lose some. And I definitely lost big time on that show!

**D**

We designed a new children's computer game called Treasures of Happy Land. I tried to come up with something that was both fun and educational, but it just didn't work out. When the game was finally released, the reviews were awful. It got one star on the AppStore. Children couldn't work out what they were supposed to do, and their parents took one look and refused to let them play it. It was a complete failure, and the producers of the show had no choice but to make me leave. I had invested so much in this project and watched it all go to waste. It just goes to show that you can't rush creativity.

**E**

I found the show to be awful and corrupt. I saw first-hand how the contestants would lie to and cheat their competitors just so they could win. We must have looked even worse to viewers after the producers made the show edits. I knew that the focus would be on drama and conflict, turning the show into a picture of human weakness. Despite making it to the semi-finals, I decided to walk out of the show, realising that the experience was not worth me sacrificing my values. I went on to start my own business, using the knowledge and skills I had gained from the show but without losing my values. My company quickly made money, and I found myself doing a lot better than I had expected.

Cambridge C1 Advanced Reading  |  Answer sheet

Name  _____          Date  _____

## Part 5
Mark the appropriate answer (A, B, C or D).                    (6 marks)

| 0 | A | B | C | D |
|---|---|---|---|---|

| 31 | A | B | C | D |   | 34 | A | B | C | D |
|----|---|---|---|---|---|----|---|---|---|---|
| 32 | A | B | C | D |   | 35 | A | B | C | D |
| 33 | A | B | C | D |   | 36 | A | B | C | D |

## Part 6
Add the appropriate answer (A–D).                    (4 marks)

| 37 | 38 | 39 | 40 |
|----|----|----|----|

## Part 7
Add the appropriate answer (A–G).                    (6 marks)

| 41 | 42 | 43 |
|----|----|----|
| 44 | 45 | 46 |

## Part 8
Add the appropriate answer (A–E).                    (10 marks)

| 47 | 48 | 49 | 50 | 51 |
|----|----|----|----|----|
| 52 | 53 | 54 | 55 | 56 |

# Answers

## Test 1

| Part 5 | | Key words from the questions | Clues from the text |
|---|---|---|---|
| 31 | C | What does Karen say about her background in paragraph 1? | ...becoming a professional garden designer was a dream come true for me...it wasn't until later in life that I realised I could do it for a living. |
| 32 | A | ...learn from the training program? | ...admits: "The program was challenging but incredibly rewarding...gained a new perspective of the natural world around me... |
| 33 | D | ...two things...succeed in the gardening business? | ...formal education, and gaining practical experience is essential for developing the skills needed to be a successful garden designer. |
| 34 | D | ...Karen suggest...show off their work? | ...I started building a catalogue of my work to show my abilities to potential clients or employers. |
| 35 | C | ...Karen...never tired of... | ...the joy and satisfaction on their faces as they walk through their newly designed garden is an experience that never gets old. |
| 36 | B | In the final paragraph, Karen talks about the physical aspects of her job in relation to... | ...end up having a good night's rest due to the physical parts of the job. |

| Part 6 | | Key words from the questions | Clues from the text |
|---|---|---|---|
| 37 | A | ...differs from the others regarding its interest in/focus on social and political change? | ...completely ignores the political and social changes ...20th century was a time of great social and political change in Britain...ignores...important historical events... |
| 38 | B | shares reviewer D's opinion on the show's well-written characters? | ...characters in the show are well-developed and complex, with both strengths and weaknesses. |
| 39 | C | ...similar view to reviewer B regarding attention to detail? | ...there's no denying that Downton Abbey is beautifully shot. The costumes and set designs are stunning, as well as extremely realistic. |
| 40 | C | ...similar opinion to reviewer A on the representation of women? | The characters are people who we mostly love or hate, and the representation of women is a bit all over the place/but many of the other women are just stereotypes. |

| Part 7 | | Key words from the questions | Clues from the text |
|---|---|---|---|
| 41 | E | Founded in 1904 by Charles Rolls and Henry Royce, the company began... | Henry Royce was an engineer...Charles Rolls was a businessman...after the two...met, they decided to create a new car company together. |
| 42 | B | Back then, it was renowned for its superior handling...and it quickly became a favourite... | In 1906, Rolls-Royce introduced the Silver Ghost, a car that would become one of the most famous models in automotive history. |
| 43 | D | However, Rolls-Royce shifted its focus once again to the aerospace industry... | During World War I, Rolls-Royce shifted its focus to producing aircraft engines for the British military....In the 1930s, the company introduced a new line of luxury cars...Rolls-Royce's success in the aerospace industry continued in the post-war period... |

| 44 | G | Rolls-Royce faced a number of challenges as the automotive industry underwent significant changes… | In 1971, the company was bought by the British government after it ran into financial difficulties…In the 1980s, Rolls-Royce faced a major challenge… |
|----|---|---|---|
| 45 | F | Luckily, Rolls-Royce was fine by… | This was costly and damaged the company's reputation. |
| 46 | C | In addition to its work in the automotive and aerospace industries… | The company has invested heavily in new technologies…explored new business models…For example, the company has been involved in the production of… |

| Part 8 | | Key words from the questions | Clues from the text |
|--------|---|---|---|
| 47 | B | …not designed to be a kind of statement | …though his signature was not initially intended to be an artistic instruction… |
| 48 | D | …combine performance and art in their work. | …incorporates elements of production art into his pieces. |
| 49 | D | …depressing sense of humour. | …art is also known for its dark humour. |
| 50 | E | They are famed for their use of text and script. | His works often uses bold, dynamic lettering and patterns… |
| 51 | A | …first to express themselves using graffiti. | …one of the first graffiti artists to use the medium as a form of personal expression. |
| 52 | E | They are able to produce work on a variety of different exteriors. | Another part of Quinones' style is his ability to adapt to different environments and surfaces. |
| 53 | C | …challenges traditional conceptions of gender roles and sexuality. | …many of his works feature homoerotic imagery that challenged conventional notions of gender and sexuality. |
| 54 | B | …required them to travel which helped them spread their art all over the city. | …who worked as a courier transporting goods in New York City…He used his job as an opportunity to show his name all over the city… |
| 55 | A | …one of the first to be nationally recognised as a graffiti artist. | …one of the first graffiti artists to achieve national attention. |
| 56 | D | …remained unknown.. | Despite many attempts to unmask the artist, his identity has remained a secret. |

## Test 2

| Part 5 | | Key words from the questions | Clues from the text |
|--------|---|---|---|
| 31 | D | …advises that you should | …and it is essential to understand this to avoid any potential legal issues. |
| 32 | C | …author say about objects passed down through the family? | …if they are valuable, you may need to consider insurance or secure storage to protect them. |
| 33 | B | If the original owner of an item has no special requirements the author suggests you… | …it is up to the person who is given the items to decide what to do with them. |

| 34 | A | When inheriting money, the author states that it is tempting to… | It is difficult not to spend the money on luxury purchases or to give it away to friends and family. |
| 35 | C | …what is the best course of action when inheriting housing? | If the property is a home, it may be necessary it may be necessary to put it up for sale or rent it. |
| 36 | D | In the final paragraph, what does the author say about responsibility? | Dealing with that responsibility well shows respect for those who have gone… |

| Part 6 | | Key words from the questions | Clues from the text |
|---|---|---|---|
| 37 | D | …shares A's opinion on how food and food production can help save the planet? | making conscious decisions…about the food they eat…These changes can be challenging, but they are necessary if we want to create a sustainable future for ourselves and future generations. One…can make is to adopt a plant-based diet. |
| 38 | A | …similar view to approach B regarding transportation and energy consumption? | …reduce our energy consumption by…using public methods of getting around or sharing a ride to work. |
| 39 | C | …differs from the others regarding their approach to saving the planet? | Environmental activism is a crucial approach to saving the planet. |
| 40 | A | …shares a similar view to approach D on the subject of waste? | …making conscious choices about the products we buy, the food we eat and the way we live our lives…energy conservation…recycling and reducing our consumption of single-use plastics. |

| Part 7 | | Key words from the questions | Clues from the text |
|---|---|---|---|
| 41 | C | As a result, the method has gained popularity worldwide and is now implemented in many schools, preschools… | This innovative approach to education focuses on creating a child-centered environment that encourages independent learning, creativity and critical thinking. |
| 42 | G | Maria's interest in education began when she worked as a doctor in a psychiatric hospital with children with disabilities. She observed that children with disabilities could learn if given the proper environment and tools. | …which she later studied at the University of Rome where she became the first woman in Italy to earn a medical degree. |
| 43 | B | One of these is the prepared environment, which is carefully designed to facilitate learning. The environment…materials that are organised and accessible to the children. | The materials are also designed to be self-correcting, allowing children to learn from their mistakes without the need for intervention from the teacher. |
| 44 | A | Children are put together, allowing them to learn from each other rather than how old they are. This approach also helps form a sense of community and encourages children to help each other. | Another characteristic of the method is the use of mixed-age groups. |
| 45 | E | In contrast, standardised education tends to prioritise teacher-led instruction, testing and a 'one-size-fits-all' approach. | The Montessori method approach also promotes creativity and a love of learning. |

| 46 | F | Another notable Montessori graduate is the Prince of Wales, who attended the Wetherby School, a Montessori school in London, England. | ...notable individuals have attended Montessori schools, including the founders of Google, Larry Page and Sergey Brin. |

| Part 8 | | Key words from the questions | Clues from the text |
| --- | --- | --- | --- |
| 47 | E | ...myths about dog behaviour that will be exposed. | Bradshaw destroys discredits common lies common myths surrounding dog behaviour... |
| 48 | D | Not many animals can communicate by understanding human gestures. | ...follow human pointing gestures, which is thought to be a key aspect of their ability to communicate and cooperate with humans. Few other animals are able to do this. |
| 49 | A | ...skills acquired when training and owning dogs. | She draws on her own experiences as a dog owner and trainer... |
| 50 | B | Looking at a dog's ears and tail movement can help assess a dog's mood. | The book contains practical tips, such as paying attention to a dog's ear and tail position... |
| 51 | C | Dogs are much more than just domesticated animals, they have their own distinctive characteristics, wants and requirements. | ...based on the idea that dogs are not just pets, but individuals with their own unique personalities. |
| 52 | E | How important bonding is between dogs and humans. | ...Bradshaw's emphasis on the importance of developing a strong relationship between dogs and their owners. |
| 53 | D | Dogs are able to translate problems just as well as infants. | ...argue that dogs possess a unique ability to understand human communication, and that their problem-solving skills are the same as those of young children. |
| 54 | A | How dogs perceive the place that they are in differently from humans. | ...examining how they perceive the world around them and how their experiences shape their behaviour...highlighting how a dog's perception of their environment is different from humans. |
| 55 | B | The complicated and somewhat misunderstood connections that dogs and humans sometimes have. | ...explores the complex and often misjudged relationship between human and dogs... |
| 56 | C | Talks about how dogs experience sadness and loss. | ...explores dogs' feelings after they lose someone. |

## Test 3

| Part 5 | | Key words from the questions | Clues from the text |
| --- | --- | --- | --- |
| 31 | B | ...while stereotypes are mostly based on false information, they usually | They are often based on limited information, although they usually have some element of truth. |
| 32 | A | ...what do people find challenging? | ...that some people find it difficult to see past stereotypes... |
| 33 | D | ...the writer say about time management and Japanese culture? | ...Japanese are known to be hard-working and disciplined, with a strong cultural emphasis on timekeeping...This stereotype may be based on the Japanese work ethic... |
| 34 | C | According to the writer, what is mainly associated with Italian culture? | Italian culture values, on the other hand, emotion and creativity... |
| 35 | A | ...asserts that African people highly rate | ...individuals value harmony and living with nature. |

| 36 | C | The writer finishes by saying a sense of community can result in | ...can lead to strong interpersonal relationships. |
|---|---|---|---|

| Part 6 | | Key words from the questions | Clues from the text |
|---|---|---|---|
| 37 | B | ...shares D's opinion on the independence of camping? | While glamping may offer more comfort and convenience, it simply cannot compare to the sense of freedom and flexibility that comes with traditional camping. |
| 38 | A | ...expresses a similar view to C regarding nature but also home comforts? | Luxury camping allows me to be outside while also enjoying the finer things in life. |
| 39 | C | ...has a different opinion than the others about moving around? | I love that I can stay in one place and not have to travel around looking for 'the perfect spot'. |
| 40 | D | ...shares a similar view to B on the challenges of the outside world? | ...embracing the difficulties. |

| Part 7 | | Key words from the questions | Clues from the text |
|---|---|---|---|
| 41 | D | But through technological advancements...understand its behaviour... routes, timings and potential reasons for its movements. | However, the blue whale's movement pattern is still not fully understood, so remote and extreme are the limits of its activities. |
| 42 | E | ...require a lot of food and must travel great distances to find enough food to survive. It is in these journeys that we find the best opportunity to monitor these kings of the sea. | ...these creatures feed on tiny fish. |
| 43 | A | The movement of blue whales is a dangerous journey with numerous hazards, as blue whales are exposed to ship strikes, fishing gear and habitat destruction. | As a result, understanding their habits are essential to conservation efforts. |
| 44 | F | One such advancement is a technology that involves attaching a small device to the whale, which can then be tracked. | Satellite has allowed researchers to track the movements of whales across vast distances. |
| 45 | B | In spite of this, they are considered to be an endangered species, with only an estimated 10,000 blue whales remaining worldwide. | They are a protected species under international law, and thankfully its population has slowly increased since the end of commercial hunting. |
| 46 | G | Even after many years in the field, I am still thrilled to witness a blue whale come out of the ocean for some air before diving to the depths again. | There is certainly more awareness now than when I started my career. |

| Part 8 | | Key words from the questions | Clues from the text |
|---|---|---|---|
| 47 | D | ...making contacts with people in the same trade and acquiring work from that? | ...find work through the connections I have made within the industry. Networking and building relationships with other musicians, promoters and venue owners has been crucial in securing gigs and collaborations. |
| 48 | A | ...figuring out how to manage both work and home? | ...finding a balance between work and life. It's easy to get caught up in the day-to-day operations of the business and forget about other aspects of life. |
| 49 | B | ...taking on a number of roles at work? | I have to wear many hats and deal with numerous responsibilities. |

| 50 | E | …spending a lot of time searching online for jobs? | I spend a lot of time on the transportation website where I find work… |
|----|---|---|---|
| 51 | A | …starting with a small amount of money and a personal computer? | In the beginning, it was just me, my laptop, and a small budget… |
| 52 | C | …work with people from different countries? | …collaborate with clients from different parts of the world. |
| 53 | B | …hiring and keeping skilled staff members? | …is finding and holding onto skilled employees…finding workers with the right skills and experience has become increasingly difficult in recent years. |
| 54 | E | …often spends the night in their place of work? | It's quite common for me to sleep in the cab of my truck. |
| 55 | E | …enjoys the relaxed atmosphere and silence? | I like the peace and quiet. |
| 56 | D | …their job being traditionally important? | …is an essential part of Spanish culture… |

## Test 4

| Part 5 | | Key words from the questions | Clues from the text |
|----|---|---|---|
| 31 | C | What does the writer say about the medicine prescribed to her? | …but I found that it only helped temporarily… |
| 32 | D | …a lack of sleep can also be an indication of… | It can also be a symptom of other medical conditions… |
| 33 | A | What advice does the writer give when talking about prescribed medicine? | …but they should be used with caution and only under the guidance of a doctor. |
| 34 | A | According to the writer, much research has been conducted on… | … have been several studies on the relationship between sleep disorders and other health conditions. |
| 35 | B | What does the writer highlight as false information? | …common myth is that a lack of sleep is just a normal part of ageing. |
| 36 | C | What is meant by the phrase 'one-size-fits-all' in the final paragraph? | …find the treatment that works best for you. |

| Part 6 | | Key words from the questions | Clues from the text |
|----|---|---|---|
| 37 | A | …expresses a similar view to C on the importance of taking breaks? | Taking regular rests can help you stay focused and avoid exhaustion. |
| 38 | B | …different opinion from D regarding the use of memory techniques? | Some people also use mnemonics…I tend to avoid this though, as for me they can also be confusing. |
| 39 | D | …similar view to B on going over work at the end of the day? | …your own quiz as a review of what you have learned and test yourself the next day. |
| 40 | D | …shares A's opinion on imitating school schedules. | …try to copy your school routine, at home. |

| Part 7 | | Key words from the questions | Clues from the text |
|---|---|---|---|
| 41 | B | It quickly became a cultural phenomenon and is still regarded as one of the best travel shows of all time. | The show followed the adventures of Michael Palin as he attempted to travel around the world in 80 days with no aeroplanes. |
| 42 | A | Despite these challenges, the show was a massive success, and Michael Palin quickly became very well-known. | …which meant that the crew had to carry heavy cameras and equipment with them as they went…Palin reflected on the experience of making the show, saying: "I can honestly say that it was one of the best experiences of my life…" |
| 43 | G | From the deserts of North Africa to the jungles of South America, Palin was always eager to experience the local way of life. | …Palin visited a variety of different countries and experienced a wide range of different cultures…It was very important to him to experience different cultures first-hand: "I think it's so important to try to understand different cultures and ways of life… |
| 44 | F | Reflecting on the show, Palin has said: "I think people still enjoy watching it because it's a reminder that there's a big wide world out there waiting to be explored. I hope the show inspires people to get out there and explore the world for themselves." | Despite the fact that the show was made over 30 years ago, it still connects with audiences today. The show is a reminder that there is so much to see and learn in the world, and that travel can be a wonderful experience. |
| 45 | C | "It is such an important part of any culture. I always make a point of trying local dishes when I travel, even if they're something I wouldn't normally eat." | …local cuisine. Palin was always eager to try new foods and flavours, and the show featured many scenes of him sampling local items. |
| 46 | D | "I think the best thing to do is to stay calm and flexible. You have to be willing to adapt to changing circumstances and be open to new experiences. Sometimes things don't go according to plan, but that's part of the adventure." | …Palin encountered many challenges and obstacles, from tackling mountain roads in Peru to dealing with corrupt officials in China. |

| Part 8 | | Key words from the questions | Clues from the text |
|---|---|---|---|
| 47 | C | …discusses one of the biggest, most thorough museums of its kind? | … it's one of the largest and most comprehensive science museums in the world. |
| 48 | B | …refers to a museum that is more interested in displaying creativity? | …specialises in decorative arts and design… |
| 49 | E | …mentions being located in a historically converted building? | The museum is located in a former power station… |
| 50 | C | …both educational and family-friendly? | …making it an ideal destination for school groups and families. |
| 51 | E | …a museum that has a wide selection of artists of varying popularity? | …home to many famous artists…as well as many lesser-known artists. |
| 52 | D | …a museum that isn't as familiar as the others? | …its relatively low profile when compared to other museums in London…waiting to be discovered by those who appreciate the beauty and elegance of decorative arts. |
| 53 | B | …a range of creative objects that covers thousands of years? | …collection of over 2.3 million objects all from various time periods. |
| 54 | A | …tries to make science and the natural world as real as possible? | …that bring the world of science and nature to life. |

| 55 | A | ...that the museum's collection of bones is notable? | Among the most notable items in the collection are the skeletons... |
| 56 | D | ...a museum with historical dress and guns on display? | ...as well as a stunning collection of military clothing and weapons... |

## Test 5

| Part 5 | | Key words from the questions | Clues from the text |
|---|---|---|---|
| 31 | C | ...people tolerated poor-quality recordings because... | ...but people put up with that since they were effectively obtaining the recording for free. |
| 32 | B | ...say about the internet in relation to new musicians? | It is more difficult to make a living. |
| 33 | A | ...if you want to succeed in the current market, they must... | One of the most important things a band can do to make it in the modern era is to be 'seen' online. |
| 34 | D | The writer refers to social media as... | ...social media has become a tool for musicians to connect with the people that like and follow them... |
| 35 | A | What does the writer say about live performances and earnings? | ...a relationship between the fans and the musicians, which can help artists make money long-term. |
| 36 | B | ...the writer says that to be successful, musicians should... | ...put in the hard work and dedication required, and be prepared to take risks to stand out. |

| Part 6 | | Key words from the questions | Clues from the text |
|---|---|---|---|
| 37 | B | ...a similar view to A regarding the representation of the main character? | The main character is a powerful and interesting figure, but her personality at times feels too simple and lazy. |
| 38 | C | ...has a similar view to D on how the book is knowledgeable about Chinese culture and history? | The author's writing is very detailed with a deep and thorough understanding of Chinese culture, traditions and history. The book is a must-read for anyone who loves rich characters and powerful, thought-provoking narratives. |
| 39 | A | ...has a different opinion than the others on the book as a whole? | This is a tedious and uninspiring novel that fails to live up to its potential. |
| 40 | B | ...shares A's opinion on how the book is a slow read? | ...the story's lack of pace and lack of action may turn off those readers looking for a more exciting read. |

| Part 7 | | Key words from the questions | Clues from the text |
|---|---|---|---|
| 41 | B | Despite its small size and relative isolation, Vanuatu has had a significant impact on global efforts to protect and preserve the natural world. | It is an archipelago consisting of 83 islands, with a total land area of approximately 12,190 square kilometres. That makes it about 20 times smaller than the UK...international conservation action. |
| 42 | F | In addition to its cultural conservation efforts, Vanuatu has also been at the front of marine conservation. | The country has established a number of protected areas, including the world's first shelter for sharks...These efforts have helped to protect the marine life that surrounds... |

| 43 | D | As a result, Vanuatu has been a leading voice in global efforts to reduce greenhouse gas emissions and promote adaptation measures to help communities cope with the impacts of climate change. | The country is particularly vulnerable to the impacts of global warming, including rising sea levels and increasingly frequent and severe storms. |
|---|---|---|---|
| 44 | C | However, the country's commitment to conservation was on full display after this, as Vanuatu worked to rebuild and restore its natural and cultural assets. | The cyclone caused widespread damage to the country's infrastructure, including its conservation areas and cultural sites. |
| 45 | G | This includes initiatives such as ecotourism, cultural tourism and community-based tourism, which can help to generate income for local communities while also promoting conservation and cultural preservation. | Rather than relying solely on traditional mass-market tourism, the government has been working to develop more sustainable forms of tourism to make money. |
| 46 | A | As the world faces increasingly urgent environmental challenges, it is essential that nations like Vanuatu continue to play a leadership role in promoting conservation and sustainable development. | The success of Vanuatu's conservation efforts…on the ongoing commitment and support of its people and leaders… broader global community…Through its cultural conservation efforts…Vanuatu has demonstrated that even small island nations can have a big impact on the global conservation agenda. |

| Part 8 | | Key words from the questions | Clues from the text |
|---|---|---|---|
| 47 | D | …new strategies during the pandemic and want to use them in their new schedule? | I'm grateful for the lessons I learned during the pandemic, and I'm confident that I can apply them to my new routine. |
| 48 | E | …positivity and determination can help beat the most difficult challenges in life. | I have learned that with a positive attitude, even the most challenging situations can be overcome. |
| 49 | A | …waste time travelling to and from work? | …I no longer have to worry about the daily commute, which saves me both time and money. |
| 50 | A | …a little anxious with regard to how they would cope with working from home? | I was nervous about how I would adapt to working from home. It was all a big rush. |
| 51 | C | …happy when the Covid-19 pandemic ended? | …I was over the moon when the pandemic was over! |
| 52 | B | …experienced little to no change? | …I have worked from home throughout most of my career, so the pandemic did not bring any significant changes to my work routine. |
| 53 | C | …difficult to get used to the technology but figured it out in the end? | It was difficult, but I managed to get the hang of it eventually. |
| 54 | E | …staying inside quite lonely due to a lack of physical contact with colleagues? | I found the isolation of remote work difficult…The lack of face-to-face communication made it challenging to build relationships and maintain a sense of team spirit. |
| 55 | C | …constantly distracted by family members? | I had two young children to look after. They were too young to understand why I had to work from home, so they kept interrupting me during the day. |
| 56 | B | …sad for those who were not used to working from home? | …I did feel sorry for people trying to manage being parents alongside working from home…I had a lot of sympathy for younger people who were missing out on their social life with friends. |

# Test 6

| Part 5 | | Key words from the questions | Clues from the text |
|---|---|---|---|
| 31 | C | In the first paragraph, the writer emphasises how melatonin… | …which is a natural chemical in our bodies, and the health implications. |
| 32 | D | The writer explains that melatonin… | … and plays an essential role in regulating the 'sleep-wake cycle'. |
| 33 | A | The writer says that a person's body patterns are affected by… | …which is influenced by external things such as light and temperature. |
| 34 | A | What does the writer say about the growth of the melatonin tablet trade? | …its production had become a billion-dollar, global business, with demand nowadays continuing to expand. |
| 35 | A | In paragraph 6, why…use 'strangely'…talk about melatonin? | …melatonin can also cause sleep disturbances in some people. |
| 36 | D | The writer says that taking melatonin tablets is not suitable… | …not advised that you take them over a long period. |

| Part 6 | | Key words from the questions | Clues from the text |
|---|---|---|---|
| 37 | C | …different experience in terms of time in the music business compared to the others? | I'm a high school student…I'm new to playing music really. I took up the guitar about two years ago… |
| 38 | B | …shares a similar opinion with D about playing live? | The feeling of going on stage though is the best part of it for me…nothing to compare to the sound of the audience cheering when you get on stage… |
| 39 | D | …shares A's negative experiences with bandmates? | I found it difficult sometimes to express myself in rehearsals and, to be honest, I think I was probably quite bossy. I had many silly arguments with bandmates. |
| 40 | A | …expresses the same opinion as B about creating music as a whole? | Playing music with others is like having a conversation. Each musician brings their own ideas and perspectives, and together we create something that is greater than most things in this world. |

| Part 7 | | Key words from the questions | Clues from the text |
|---|---|---|---|
| 41 | F | Lawrence was an exceptional student and received a scholarship to study at Jesus College in the UK, where he did very well in medieval history and archaeology. | After graduation, Lawrence worked as an archaeologist in the Middle East… |
| 42 | A | However, Lawrence's true usefulness became clear in 1916 when he was sent to Arabia to work with the Arab Revolt against the Ottoman Empire. | …proved himself to be very skilled, using his knowledge of Arabic and his understanding of Arab culture to gather valuable information ..played a key role in organising and leading his army. |
| 43 | B | Some British officers saw him as someone who operated alone and did not follow traditional military tactics. | Despite his successes, Lawrence was not without his criticisms. |

| 44 | C | However, he was disappointed with the final outcome of the agreement, feeling that the Arab people had not been given the independence they deserved. | He was heavily involved in negotiating the Arab-British Treaty of 1922, which recognised the independence of several Arab states and established British influence in the region. |
|---|---|---|---|
| 45 | E | It became a bestseller and is still considered one of the greatest personal books of the 20th century… | …a new career as a writer. He wrote several books… |
| 46 | G | It was a shock to his family, friends and admirers all over the world. | Lawrence died on May 19, 1935, at the age of 46, in a motorcycle accident. |

| Part 8 | | Key words from the questions | Clues from the text |
|---|---|---|---|
| 47 | B | …something that presented information on methods of production in the past? | …provided insights into the manufacturing processes. |
| 48 | D | …to help the authorities solve a case? | I am confident that the work will be of great value to the police. |
| 49 | E | …that may have attracted people from other places? | …would have been a place of worship for the local Roman population, and perhaps even a place for other people to visit from other parts of the empire. |
| 50 | A | …reshaped the historical relationships between two countries? | It was an incredible discovery, one that would rewrite the history of Scotland's relationship with the Roman Empire. |
| 51 | C | …research in many different countries and is included in educational papers? | Our work will be published in academic journals and shared with scholars around the world, contributing to our collective understanding of the region's history. |
| 52 | E | …graduated recently and is happy to work? | As a newly qualified archaeologist fresh out of education… |
| 53 | E | …found something unexpectedly due to construction work? | …that discovered a Roman temple in a field that was scheduled to have a road built through it. |
| 54 | D | …that humans occupied the area prior to what was initially believed? | This is of great significance, if true, as it suggests that the area was inhabited by humans much earlier than previously thought. |
| 55 | A | …was in charge of the project? | I was leading a team… |
| 56 | C | …talks about how much we still don't know? | …is an important reminder of how much we have yet to learn about our past… |

## Test 7

| Part 5 | | Key words from the questions | Clues from the text |
|---|---|---|---|
| 31 | C | …AI could take over a number of jobs…important to see that… | …new opportunities for employment…arise…result of the growth of AI. |

| 32 | A | In paragraph 2…three jobs that demand… | …a high level of technical understanding… |
|---|---|---|---|
| 33 | D | What does the writer say about data science and businesses? | Data science is a field that is rapidly growing in popularity, as businesses look to extract valuable insights from vast amounts of data. |
| 34 | B | What made Sarah want to study computer science? | …and really enjoyed finding solutions to puzzles and technical dilemmas throughout school. |
| 35 | A | … sixth paragraph, what…Sarah's goal? | …a leadership role…be part of the future of technology. |
| 36 | C | In the final paragraph, what advice does the writer give once you start studying? | Once you're at university, see which areas of AI you enjoy the most and look for opportunities for further studies. |

| Part 6 | | Key words from the questions | Clues from the text |
|---|---|---|---|
| 37 | A | …expresses the same opinion as B…specific choice of language. | …with a focus on dialogue and distinctive use of words. |
| 38 | D | …differs from the others…overall opinion of the book? | However, I was disappointed with what I found. |
| 39 | C | …shares a similar view to C regarding the significance of the book? | … a worthy addition to the genre of crime fiction… |
| 40 | C | …expresses the same opinion as D…impact of other crime writers? | …two of the most famous authors of this genre, can be seen throughout The Black Apple… |

| Part 7 | | Key words from the questions | Clues from the text |
|---|---|---|---|
| 41 | A | Despite this, public healthcare systems…under attack …threatens the well-being…people…must be stopped. | …every citizen, regardless of their income or social status, has access to healthcare services when they need them. |
| 42 | D | In contrast…The United States…private healthcare system… | …poor and working-class citizens are not left behind…can receive adequate medical attention just as the wealthy do. |
| 43 | E | Groups here…active in supporting public healthcare…the cost of healthcare…United States continues to rise… | Despite these efforts…United States has yet to implement a public healthcare system… |
| 44 | C | Contrast this with…pay for Covid-19 testing and treatment. This meant that… | The NHS was able to provide free testing…treatment for all Covid-19 patients… |
| 45 | F | The campaign's slogan…emphasises the health benefits of reducing alcohol consumption. | The campaign, called 'Count 14', wants to reduce the number of alcohol units consumed by adults to 14 or fewer per week. |
| 46 | B | …everyone receives the healthcare they need…The Covid-19 pandemic has shown that public healthcare systems are the most effective… | …public healthcare systems…vital to ensure…all citizens have access…healthcare…regardless…financial status. |

| Part 8 | | Key words from the questions | Clues from the text |
|---|---|---|---|
| 47 | D | ...worked in a school before competing in the local election? | As a retired headmaster...I am running for office in the upcoming local election. |
| 48 | E | ...focuses on the development of transportation? | I will also work to improve the infrastructure in our town, such as train links, high-speed internet and public amenities, |
| 49 | A | ...in local campaigns related to the environment? | Over the years, I have been actively involved in various environmental campaigns. |
| 50 | B | ...centre of town enjoyable for everybody? | My goal is to make our town centre the heart of our community, a place where people can come together to shop, dine and socialise. |
| 51 | C | ...infrastructure for those with issues moving around freely? | I want to highlight the issue of accessibility at our town's train station...not fully accessible for people with disabilities, particularly those who use wheelchairs. |
| 52 | A | ...the reduction of air pollution? | ...to develop practical solutions to reduce our carbon footprint, improve air quality. |
| 53 | E | ...increasing employment will lead to an improvement in the economy? | ...encourage more businesses to open in our town, which will create economic growth and prosperity that will benefit us all. |
| 54 | D | ...from their previous job can help them if elected? | These skills and experiences are directly applicable to the challenges facing our community today. |
| 55 | C | ...create a warmer and more global environment for everybody? | ...create a welcoming and inclusive environment for all... |
| 56 | A | ...the environment by motivating people to leave their cars at home? | In the past, I was involved with a very successful transport scheme that encouraged people to stop driving and start using public transport. |

## Test 8

| Part 5 | | Key words from the questions | Clues from the text |
|---|---|---|---|
| 31 | A | What two things... highlight...necessary...a barista? | ...requires a unique combination of skills, knowledge and passion. |
| 32 | D | Why does the writer highlight the importance of the barista arriving early? | ...as coffee shops are usually busiest in the morning when people are on their way to work or starting their day. |
| 33 | B | Why...important for a barista to pay attention to their customers? | ...make recommendations based on their tastes. |
| 34 | D | ...making small talk is important because... | This is a key part of the job, as it helps to create a welcoming atmosphere in the coffee shop. |
| 35 | B | According to the writer, an unclean environment can affect the coffee's... | A dirty shop...can affect the flavour of the coffee. |

| 36 | C | What should a barista do when their shift finishes? | ...tidies the coffee station, ensuring that it is ready for the next morning. |

| Part 6 | | Key words from the questions | Clues from the text |
|---|---|---|---|
| 37 | A | ...shares...same experiences as D...conflict with siblings? | ...I often felt like I was being picked on by my brothers, who would tease and exclude me, and make fun of me... |
| 38 | D | ...has the same view as C...being spoilt? | ...favourite when growing up. She loved me and showered me with affection and attention. |
| 39 | A | ...has a different opinion than the others...having siblings? | Overall, I would prefer to be an only child. |
| 40 | C | ...shares a similar view to B about family members altering their mood? | ...that I needed my parents... attention to make me feel happy. |

| Part 7 | | Key words from the questions | Clues from the text |
|---|---|---|---|
| 41 | C | ...what...the effects that social media and the internet have on our social lives...mental health and well-being? | While the internet and social media platforms...easy to connect with people all over the world...led to a decline in our face-to-face interactions, making us less social beings. |
| 42 | G | However...communication has become much more convenient and accessible. | We can now easily share updates, photos and messages with our friends and family at the touch of a button... |
| 43 | F | ...because...different...downside of online social networks...pressure...users...appear popular... | Social media and the 'friendships'...must be separated from the traditional idea of being social and having friendships. |
| 44 | B | Studies have shown...people who spend more time online and on social media platforms...more likely to experience...loneliness than those who engage in face-to-face interactions. | Despite the many advantages that social media and the internet have brought, there is growing concern... |
| 45 | A | Research has also shown ...people who spend more time on social media are more likely to experience...anxiety, depression and low self-esteem. | This has led to a decrease in our ability to read and interpret social signals...However, it is important to note that social media... |
| 46 | E | Through social media, individuals can connect with others who share their beliefs and work together to effect positive change in their communities and in society... | Furthermore, social media can be a powerful tool for raising awareness about important social and political issues... |

| Part 8 | | Key words from the questions | Clues from the text |
|---|---|---|---|
| 47 | B | ...no clue what to do at the start of the show? | First off, I had no idea what I was doing... |
| 48 | E | ...left the show due to personal and moral conflicts? | I decided to walk out of the show, realising that the experience was not worth sacrificing my values for. |

| 49 | A | …they were more intelligent than everybody else on the show? | They were all a bunch of amateurs who couldn't handle my superior intellect and business brain. |
|---|---|---|---|
| 50 | B | …whole thing was more difficult than it seemed? | And I learned that organising a fashion show is not as easy as it looks! |
| 51 | E | …create their own company? | I went on to start my own business, using the knowledge and skills I had gained from the show. |
| 52 | C | …respect the views and opinions of their teammates? | I decided that the rest of my team didn't have a clue, so I completely ignored all of their advice. |
| 53 | D | …received terrible feedback from customers? | …the reviews were terrible. It got one star on the AppStore. |
| 54 | A | …shocked when they were kicked off the show by their teammates? | I wasn't surprised when my teammates decided that they wanted me to leave. |
| 55 | C | …handled things quite well? | …I thought I had it all under control… |
| 56 | D | …put a lot of money and time into the assignment? | I had invested so much into this project and watched it all go to waste. |

Printed and bound by CPI Group (UK) Ltd, Croydon, CR0 4YY

13/05/2025

01869813-0001